ECKANKAR
KEY TO SOUL TRAVEL

ECKANKAR
KEY TO SOUL TRAVEL

HAROLD KLEMP

ECKANKAR
Minneapolis
Eckankar.org

ECKANKAR—Key to Soul Travel

Copyright © 2003, 2022 ECKANKAR

This book has been excerpted and adapted from *Past Lives, Dreams, and Soul Travel*, by Harold Klemp, copyright © 2003 ECKANKAR.

All rights reserved. The terms ECKANKAR, ECK, EK, MAHANTA, SOUL TRAVEL, and VAIRAGI, among others, are trademarks of ECKANKAR, PO Box 2000, Chanhassen, MN 55317-2000 USA.

240106

Printed in USA

Photo of Sri Harold Klemp by Art Galbraith

ISBN: 978-1-57043-563-8

Library of Congress Cataloging-in-Publication Data

Names: Klemp, Harold, author. | Klemp, Harold. Past lives, dreams, and soul travel.
Title: Eckankar : key to soul travel / Harold Klemp.
Other titles: Key to soul travel
Description: Minneapolis : Eckankar, [2024] | "This book has been excerpted and adapted from Past lives, dreams, and soul travel by Harold Klemp, copyright ©2003 ECKANKAR"--Title page verso. | Summary: "Author Harold Klemp, spiritual leader of Eckankar, shares stories of people who have left their physical body and returned to tell about it. People who have experienced the freedom and joy beyond the physical world"-- Provided by publisher.
Identifiers: LCCN 2024010186 | ISBN 9781570435638 (paperback)
Subjects: LCSH: Eckankar (Organization) | Reincarnation. | Dreams. | Astral projection.
Classification: LCC BP605.E3 K55367 2024 | DDC 299/.93--dc23/eng/20240412
LC record available at https://lccn.loc.gov/2024010186

∞ This paper meets the requirements of ANSI/NISO Z39.48-1992 (Permanence of Paper).

Contents

Introduction 1

1. Soul Travel—Voyages into the Higher Worlds 11

2. Learning to Soul Travel 35

3. Beyond Soul Travel: Seeing, Knowing, and Being 53

4. The Light and Sound of God 67

5. Spiritual Exercises for Soul Travel 95

6. By the Way 135

About the Author 139

Next Steps in Spiritual Exploration .. 141

For Further Reading 144

Glossary 147

Introduction

A certain belief was drummed into me as a boy about life after death. It was the idea that at death Soul "sleeps" until the final day of judgment, that death marks a time of complete unconsciousness. But this notion rang like a wooden sleigh bell.

To me, such a state of death afforded the horrors of a nightmare.

I grew up on a farm. Family life meant raising and caring for horses, cattle, hogs, chickens, cats, and a couple of dogs, as well as planting crops to feed them and us. But just as important, our family felt a pull toward our church on Sundays for spiritual food. Church was at once a religious and a social center. Of course, all came to worship God, but the day's spice was the after-worship visit with neighbors outside the church doors.

Men weighed in on land, cattle, crops, or local issues. Women scarfed up tidbits about family, health, cooking, or their kids at school. Boys kidded each other, while girls shared their own brand of concerns or silliness.

However, few discussed religion. The church service was over.

Nearly everyone in church was part of some bigger family circle. It was natural, then, that everyone knew everyone else, so a church service was a reunion of friends and relatives.

During those years, Grandpa and Grandma often lived on the family farm with one of their adult children. The grandparents, wise and beloved elders, helped care for the grandchildren, did light chores, but still rode herd on their grown children. In time, of course, the old ones would pass on one by one. The day of such a one's funeral was like a Sunday in that farmers did the bare morning and evening chores, milking cows and cleaning the barn.

A Soul's passing was thus a day of worship, yet one of sadness too.

Children were on hand the days or weeks before a grandparent's passing. The process of dying had not yet become sanitized and hidden away as it is today, when the sick and elderly go to age and die away from home. The fact of dying happened right before our eyes. We saw death on many occasions.

While death meant the loss of someone near and dear to us, it was not the mysterious vanishing of an elder seen but once or twice a year on some festive occasion.

More than that, a rural child watched parents and neighbors prepare for the funeral. He overheard them on the phone. They called each other to express sorrow, offer consolation, and perhaps give a gentle commentary about the good character of the departed—whether true or not.

The final good-byes came at church. Whole families, from baby to most feeble elder, attended the funeral service if health and weather allowed. Our congregation first listened to the pastor give the funeral blessings. Then, the entire assembly filed out to the cemetery by the church where the coffin's vault sank into a dark, gloomy hole and the piles of fresh earth were tidied over with green ground cloths. We boys stayed to watch four assigned farmers shovel the grave shut. Last, we raced to the church basement for a hearty meal of fellowship prepared by the Ladies Aid Society.

It was at such country funerals that doubts sprang to mind about the "sleep" state of an individual at death. Everyone in church made the assumption that the human body and Soul body were one and the same.

Years later, I learned of other thoughts on the matter. ECKANKAR taught the fact of Soul's ability to leave the body in full consciousness at time of death.

Yes, the church held to its dark philosophy. The physical body, it said, would decay and serve as worm food, but on the Last Day a more glorious body would rise from the grave. That would mark Soul's victory over death.

But these tenets lent me little peace of mind.

What kid wouldn't have traded an eye-tooth for a ringside seat at the cemetery on that last, great day? What a chance to catch the spectacle of a lifetime. Graves opening, and seeing all those people helping each other out of the ground? A splendid show. (Better than a county fair!)

Yet for all the promise of excitement, an ominous cloud threw its shadow over this one-of-a-kind presentation. What were the odds of this spectacle taking place in my lifetime? A million to one? No, a trillion. That left a most unhappy prospect. Would I be another of the billions and billions of unlucky Souls trapped in a dark prison hole for a thousand or ten thousand years? Not a bright and cheery picture for a kid with claustrophobia.

Moreover, what if something went wrong with the resurrection plan? Could it fail? What if I failed to awaken from the sleep of death?

Mistakes do happen.

So over time, funerals got more and more of my attention. You could say I was in search of a more secure plan for the afterlife.

I thus became a seeker.

Indeed, an awakening did occur as I grew from boy to young man. This awakening had stolen into my awareness like the first dim rays of a summer dawn and then burst into full glory some years later.

An early perception of God's love and grace had blessed me as a child. Like, what was that mysterious humming sound at night when I was two and three? My brother, two years older, and I still had a bed in the bedroom of our parents, so when my tiny voice pierced the darkness it awoke everyone.

"What is that?"

But neither Mother, Dad, nor brother could hear what I heard. When I tried to explain the "what" as a humming sound, they said, "It's only the electric wires outside. Now go to sleep." Dad's alarm would clatter at four o'clock in the morning to rouse him for chores. He had no time for nonsense from a kid.

Yet as the years rolled on, my thoughts at night would at times return to those early childhood memories of the mysterious humming sound. It had made me feel light, full, and good. Where had it gone? The electric wires still ran outside my window, but that soothing, almost musical, humming sound was gone for good, no doubt.

How wrong I was.

Later, in ECKANKAR, I learned that this humming sound was one of the many currents of God. It was part of the movement of God's Voice—the Holy Spirit, or ECK—vibrating the ethers of time and space to a level some ears could hear. Like, say, those of a child.

To listen to one of the sacred sounds is a great joy and spiritual blessing.

Anyway, a lot of gentle or stormy clouds had crossed the canopy of my life before that revelation about the humming's origin came to me. In the meantime, there were other awakenings too. Little ones, in looking back. Yet each was all I could accept at a given level of unfoldment. These awakenings included visions, dreams of past lives and the future, Soul Travel, and other spiritual experiences that left me wonder struck and sometimes even terror stricken.

Yet they spoke of the mysteries of the Eternal One, God, the Creator.

These small awakenings were directed at one goal: to find spiritual freedom in this lifetime. Here and now. There was no reason to enter a "death sleep" that could last for centuries, and maybe forever. What if my childhood religion had it wrong? There were a lot of other religions out there with conflicting beliefs. If my church had the wrong take on the life hereafter, I would wait in the grave a long time.

The joke would be on me.

* * *

You are at that point, too, where some Voice of God has shaken you awake from a deep spiritual slumber.

I think you'll like the stories in these pages by people like you. You'll hear others tell a compelling story about a past life, a dream, or a Soul Travel journey that reveals the all-caring nature of God's love. This love works wonders.

Within this precious book are the voices of seekers like you, people also on the most direct path to spiritual understanding and freedom—here and now.

Welcome!

1
Soul Travel—Voyages into the Higher Worlds

*D*aydreams, night dreams, contemplation, Soul Travel—all are steps in the pursuit of heaven.

In ECKANKAR, an earnest seeker is under the protection of a spiritual guide known as the MAHANTA. This is the Spiritual Traveler. As the MAHANTA he is the Inner Master, the one who comes on the other planes to impart knowledge, truth, and wisdom. But he also has an outer side. Here he is the Living ECK Master.

Thus, the spiritual leader of ECKANKAR—the MAHANTA, the Living ECK Master—is both an inner and outer teacher for all who wish to learn more of God and life. Such is his role.

So as spiritual guide, the Master helped an African man—via the Ancient Science of Soul Travel—enjoy a reunion with his deceased son.

This man had a teenage son. When the youth was but fifteen years of age, he stepped on a sharp object, got tetanus, and soon died. The father, an ECKist, wished to meet his son on the inner planes. So he went into contemplation and chanted the sacred word *HU* to get spiritual aid. During this contemplation, the MAHANTA let him move into the Soul body and find his son through Soul Travel.

Father and son thus greeted each other with great joy and love in heaven.

Then the man asked his son a question that had long plagued him: "How did you hurt yourself? What did you step on that gave you tetanus?"

The youth said, "In the corner of the passageway that leads to the kitchen is a nail. That is what I stepped on."

When the father awoke from contemplation, he rose from his bed and examined the passageway. Indeed, in a dark corner near the kitchen, a rusty nail jutted from a floorboard. It was off to the side, but the teen had had the misfortune to step on its deadly tip. The man wrenched the lethal nail from the floor to ensure that no other life would be at risk.

So even while he felt deep anguish from his son's death, this Soul Travel experience let him see for himself that his son lived on in peace and happiness.

Soul Travel is a gift of heaven.

Like-Minded Souls

Many who embrace the ECK teachings today have in one way or another had some spiritual experiences that their fellows have not. Among them may be near-death experiences, out-of-the-body adventures, Soul Travel, astral projection, or even visions.

In most cases, though, it's better that people not have such experiences day in and day out. Individuals who do are often unable to handle them. In general, they spin out of control, wobbling in their spiritual orbits, causing trouble for themselves and others.

For most people, psychic or spiritual experiences catch them by surprise. They often happen before one has heard of ECKANKAR. But they do awaken a seeker. With a sense of wonder and self-doubt, he may ask, *What happened? Am I losing my mind?*

So he turns to some authority figure to find an answer to the gnawing questions about his unusual experience. "What happened?" he says. The minister doesn't know. Doctors of philosophy, psychology, or one of the medical arts return blank looks too.

Where to now?

Then one day he watches a TV show and learns of others with an extraordinary experience like his own.

"Ah," he says, "all these experiences sound true."

Now our seeker wonders, *Where can I meet people like me?*

Often it's hard to make contact. The TV subjects are from points around the country, and the TV program may not give out names or addresses for reasons of privacy.

But there is a chance to meet others of like experience.

ECKANKAR is here. Among its benefits is the chance for like-minded people to meet at public seminars. At this open forum, all may learn more of the divine plan behind a variety of inner experiences. The ancient ECK teachings are now available. An advantage of ECKANKAR and the ECK seminars is that they provide a common meeting ground for all who have had a life-changing experience.

One in three Americans admits to a remarkable experience—either of leaving the physical body or some other phenomenon. Few may have understood its nature, but nonetheless, no one can shake them of a belief in its reality. We of ECKANKAR are here to help them understand. The ECK talks and writings open a window to the mysteries of the higher worlds and what such an experience means.

What Is Soul Travel?

In the simplest terms, Soul Travel is an individual moving closer to the heart of God. This movement takes a variety of forms.

Soul Travel is, for the most part, a tool for use in the worlds below the Soul Plane, first of the true spiritual worlds. It takes one through the Astral, Causal, Mental, and Etheric Planes. As a whole, these are the planes of time and space. Soul Travel occurs in two general ways. One form is the sensation of fast movement of the Soul body through the planes of time and space. In reality, though, is such movement possible?

You see, Soul exists on all planes, so

what feels like movement, or travel, is simply Soul coming into an agreement with fixed states and conditions that already exist in some world of time and space.

If you can imagine a scene, then you can be there this same instant in the Soul body. That is the Imaginative technique. It may feel as though you are hurtling through space at a breakneck speed, like a rocket, and zooming on a journey to outer space. In fact, though, Soul (you) is motionless. It is shifting Its attention to some higher state. That shifting of attention results in a feeling of fast motion to the material senses.

Soul Travel begins with a Spiritual Exercise of ECK in a physical setting.

A contemplative may hear a rushing sound, like a wailing wind in a tunnel, along with a sensation of incredible speed. But as explained, Soul doesn't move; Soul *is*. Time and space adjust to Soul's state of consciousness, and it is this adjustment of time and space that renders an illusion of movement or breathtaking speed. A seeming, rapid change of location is one aspect of Soul Travel that may prove to be a daunting obstacle for the timid. These people fear going beyond themselves.

Soul Travel is, therefore, for the bold and courageous in spirit. But remember, since one doesn't in fact travel anywhere, it's impossible to get lost.

Keep that principle in mind during a spiritual exercise. It will lend the confidence to open your heart to love and so delight in any enlightenment that finds you.

Another form of Soul Travel is the expansion of consciousness. This aspect is the true state of personal revelation or enlightenment that we aspire to in ECK. It visits both the timid and the bold, and is a gentler, less robust version of movement in consciousness. Most people experience this sort of gradual shifting of awareness.

Love and wonder define Soul Travel the best.

Golden Kiss of God

Soul Travel is thus of several dimensions. Some people describe it as a shift in consciousness. Out of the blue, some event happens to shed light on a spiritual matter that had mystified them. A shift in consciousness to a new plane flits in like a soft, golden kiss of God. Then, these lucky Souls *know* they've had the best of good fortune and have touched the hem of divine love. Rather, it has brushed them.

Soul Travel, as stated, may also be of a more dramatic sort. In this case, an individual transcends the human body and tastes the love and freedom that are a birthright. He rises into the other worlds. Each experience fits him, because each is but a reflection of his spiritual state.

People ask, "Why is it so important in ECKANKAR to learn Soul Travel?"

Soul Travel, in a broad sense, is of much value because it is a link to the expansion of consciousness. The rule of destiny holds that people at some time will begin to awaken to who and what they are. A knowledge of past lives may also open to them by way of dreams or déjà vu. A few catch a glimpse of future events.

Note that Soul Travel means moving into the higher realms of God, to places people haven't yet dreamed of. Soul Travel reveals a majesty and security that abounds in the arms of God alone.

For this reason, Soul Travel transcends astral or mind travel, and rote prayer, elevating one into profound spiritual areas. Whenever Soul reaches the far orbits of the inner planes through Soul Travel, the human heart opens to God's all-consuming love.

It is our very purpose to discover that love.

A GENTLE EXERCISE BEFORE SLEEP

To travel to your inner worlds, try this spiritual exercise. Do it each evening before sleep. Shut your eyes, then sing

HU or your secret word for five or ten minutes. (A secret word comes with the Second Initiation. An individual may request this initiation after two years of study in the ECK discourses.)

Right before dozing off, say to the MAHANTA, "Please take me to the place where I can learn all that is good for my unfoldment. Take me to a Temple of Golden Wisdom."

Or say, "Let me see what it's like to Soul Travel; you have permission to help me."

Let a feeling of warmth and goodness fill your heart. The MAHANTA is a trusted friend and companion who loves you as you love him. Be assured of his love, protection, and guidance.

You will be safe in every way.

Seekers in ages past discovered and followed a teacher who could guide them beyond the spiritual limitations of body and mind. Countless others, including many saints, have mastered the art and science of Soul Travel.

It is in your hands to become adept at it too.

* * *

Julie gets an inside scoop on the Tin Man from The Wizard of Oz. *Lauretta misses the 1981 World Wide of ECK, but learn how she meets the new Master. Both stories appear in* Earth to God, Come In Please. . ., *books 1 and 2.*

Finding a Heart of Gold

By Julie Olson

A child of twelve, I had a dream. I was standing in the cemetery near home. One by one, I looked at the children's graves—flat marble slabs the size of shoebox lids lying level with the ground.

Suddenly I spied an intensely bright gold coin glittering in the dry brown grass. As I stooped to pick it up, I saw other coins scattered in an abundant trail across the lawn. I collected many of them to take home, feeling rich and full of glee. As I picked them up, the trail of gold coins led me out of the cemetery. The dream ended.

The next day, I went to the graveyard after school, half-hoping to glimpse a real gold coin. The dream stayed with me but had no real meaning until almost twenty years later.

* * *

In September of 1986, an unchecked infection raged through my kidneys and bloodstream. My husband and I were living in a new section of our large city, and my physician was out of town. When my temperature reached 106 degrees, my husband took me to a hospital that offered emergency care.

The next four days were a nightmare. The hospital was overcrowded and understaffed. (It later came under federal investigation for incompetent care.) The doctor was unfamiliar with my medical history and couldn't diagnose my problem. I developed a life-threatening case of pneumonia that went completely undetected. I lay in the hospital approaching death, surrounded by medical knowledge and technology.

Each day I thought, *This can't get worse.*

But each day it did. The improper care, ineffectual medicine, and overcrowded room were all part of a carefully crafted divine plan. It wasn't apparent at the time, but I was right where I belonged.

I was never quite conscious. Instead, I felt myself hovering around or above my physical body, not wanting to feel the constant pain and discomfort. Having studied the teachings of ECKANKAR for fourteen years, I never lost that all-important link with the Inner Master. The illness and pain tried to absorb all my attention, but the loving presence of the MAHANTA, my spiritual guide, wafted in and out of my consciousness.

It gave me great comfort and security.

However, I began to ask Spirit why I was not getting the right medical attention. What had landed me in this crazy hospital? My husband and parents felt much alarm, since I'd lost the strength to lift my arms. It was hard to breathe. Clearly, I was near death.

Helpless and weak, too ill to demand anything, I couldn't even focus my attention to chant *HU*, the ancient name for God. Occasionally, just the *H* and *U* would flash together in my inner vision like a neon sign.

On the fourth morning I began to sink. I could feel myself loosening the grip on physical reality and stopped struggling at that point to surrender all.

"Anything is better than this, MAHANTA. If I am ready to leave, I will go."

My mind cleared for the first time, and an inner calm descended. It was evident I was close to translating (dying). My body felt like a broken, feverish husk, of no further use. And yet there was a powerful current flowing through me that was not physical. Soul was calm, peaceful, observing, and detached.

As I rose above the pain, I recognized a familiar feeling like floating. I'd felt it many times before during the Spiritual Exercises of ECK and knew I was out of my body—perhaps this time never to return. I kept saying to the Inner Master, "I am ready, I am ready."

There was no emotion, no pull toward family or loved ones, just calm expectancy.

So this is dying, I thought.

Then, as if someone had flicked on a movie projector, I saw a scene from the classic movie *The Wizard of Oz*. It registered in absolute clarity upon my vision—every note of the music in perfect pitch and clear, every detail in vivid color far beyond the reaches of Metro-Goldwyn-Mayer.

In the movie, Dorothy finds the Tin Man rusting away in the woods, locked into one position as the years passed. She oils his joints. The sheer joy of movement makes the Tin Man dance. I watched every nuance of the Tin Man's movements, felt every musical note, as pure happiness animated his clunky body.

His joy is unhampered by the awkward shell he wears.

The Tin Man's song is "If I Only Had a Heart." He pleads with Dorothy to take him to the Land of Oz so he can ask the Wizard for a heart, because his creator forgot to give him one.

Every word of the song registered deeply. The scene faded at the end of his song.

As I returned to my physical body, tears rolled down my cheeks. *I* was the Tin Man—encased in a hard shell of physical, emotional, and mental rust. This rust was karma—a shell of pain that had built up through lifetimes of heartbreak and disappointment. Now it was keeping me from my true heart—as Soul.

I asked the Inner Master to help me

open my heart to Spirit in this life.

Only the ECK Life Force could soften the karmic rust of centuries. This rust had collected over many incarnations, dating as far back as Atlantis. My heart had been broken so many times as I failed important spiritual tests.

The scene changed, and I was standing in a mist.

Something began to take shape before me, and I became aware of a large, round table. I seated myself at it, alongside several ECK Masters of the VAIRAGI Order.

Sri Harold Klemp was immediately recognizable, as were Rebazar Tarzs and Fubbi Quantz. A discussion began. I couldn't hear the actual words, but there was a vibration or hum which signaled their conference. I knew the conversation was about me. Presently the discussion stopped, and a question entered my consciousness.

"Julie, what do you want to do?"

A feeling of great love, patience, and

compassion surrounded me as their question sank in. Did I want to leave the physical body now? The choice, as Soul, was mine alone.

Two thoughts cropped up so fast my mind didn't have time to censor them. Soul, the observer, was speaking. One thought was a concern over my husband's anguish and pain. We'd been married only four months. The second thought: I haven't yet met the Soul who just joined our family, which is very important to me. (My sister had just had a baby.)

At that moment my fate was sealed. There was no chance to mentalize the choice; it was made beyond the mind. Soul, the golden heart, had made Its choice. Feeling a sudden surge of purpose and strength, I returned with a rush to my body.

Things moved quickly after that. Within an hour my regular doctor phoned. I was released into his care at another hospital.

The ambulance ride was a lonely one. I felt the weight of my decision as the reality of the physical universe closed in around me. The bouncy ride, the wailing siren, the narrow gurney I was strapped to—all stood in stark contrast to my spiritual visions of the morning. I felt painfully alone.

Ironically, a deep fear of death clutched my heart.

Just then, the ambulance attendant began to sing. Softly at first and then louder, part lullaby and part hymn. I immediately felt the presence of the MAHANTA and relaxed. I couldn't see the attendant (and for all he knew I was unconscious), but his soothing voice drowned out the wail of the siren. His unselfconscious song carried the healing force of the divine Sound Current.

I'm so weak, I thought, *I couldn't ask him to continue should he stop.* But he kept on singing.

When we arrived at the new hospital, I was caught up in a whirl of activity as my body was hooked up to various machines and tubes. I remained in the intensive care unit for three weeks. It took a full twelve months to regain my health.

The Living ECK Master declared that The Year of Spiritual Healing for the chelas of ECKANKAR—and many other searching Souls.

* * *

The childhood dream of golden coins returned and stayed with me.

It was a promise made long ago by Spirit. In this life, Soul would be freed by the MAHANTA from the dead traps of ignorance. The karma of many lifetimes would dissolve—lifetimes where I had lost all resonance with myself as Soul. Each golden coin in my dream symbolized a secret gift from the ECK— a key insight into life. These insights would lead me out of the constant round of birth, death, and rebirth, out of the physical plane (the cemetery).

Soul was free of Its earthly bonds.

ECKANKAR is the path I have chosen to help me gather the golden coins of wisdom in my path. I have the deepest gratitude to the VAIRAGI Masters and to Sri Harold Klemp, the current MAHANTA, the Living ECK Master, for showing me how to use them to open myself as Soul.

I guess you could say the Tin Man found his heart of gold.

The God Worlds of ECK

By Lauretta McCoy

It was the weekend of the 1981 World Wide of ECK, and I was disappointed at being unable to attend. But being a creative Soul, I promised myself during a spiritual exercise to visit the seminar in the dream state or through Soul Travel.

That night I had a dream.

I was standing in a place of soft white light when a man drove up in a beautiful, antique, black Model T Ford.

It was in mint condition.

Wow! I thought, *I really love this car.*

The car in my dream had a certain mystique. It was timeless, better than any modern-day car, and like Soul, nothing could keep it from its journey or destiny. The driver of the car approached me. Greeting each other, we expressed our admiration for the black Model T. He was an average-looking man about my height, dressed in a suit.

"You want to go for a ride?" he asked.

My heart stopped. Just the thought of riding in this car was beyond my wildest dreams. My heart said yes, but doubt crept in. I studied him.

Who is this man? I don't know him.

"No," I said.

But he didn't seem bothered by my answer and sensed what was in my heart. Taking my hand in his, he said in a kind voice, "Come on and take a ride."

The invitation was extended with much love. I looked at his gentle face, and all doubt faded. I knew it would be all right to go for a ride. Before we climbed into the Model T, he motioned me to follow him to the rear of the car and pointed to a bumper sticker.

It read The God Worlds of ECK.

"Wow! The God Worlds of ECK!" I said, and immediately woke up.

What a wonderful dream, I thought.

A few days later, my friends returned from the 1981 World Wide of ECK in great excitement. ECKANKAR had a new Living ECK Master. One of my million questions was, "What does he look like?" No one seemed able to describe him.

Finally, I drove to the ECK Center to see for myself what the new Living ECK Master looked like. There it was, a picture of the kind gentleman who had offered me a ride to the God Worlds of ECK in his beautiful Model T Ford. It was Sri Harold Klemp, the MAHANTA, the Living ECK Master.

I knew he was truly the new Living ECK Master, able to help me grow and explore the inner worlds of God.

2
Learning to Soul Travel

*Ann, let's say, lived in an apartment. She had learned to Soul Travel in her dreams but often wondered why she never traveled beyond her apartment building.

Each time Ann fell asleep and awoke in the Soul body, she could see her physical body lying on the bed. Her routine was to walk through her front door and out into the hallway of the building. There she'd wait. By and by, the Inner Master would appear from around the corner.

"Where do you want to go?" he'd say.

Her usual answer was, "I want to go to a Golden Wisdom Temple." Yet the apartment building was the extent of her Soul Travel journeys.

One night she asked the Inner Master why she never left her living quarters in her dreams. "Please show me what I need to do."

"How did you learn to Soul Travel?" he asked.

So she began thinking about the first time she had found herself out of the body.

Finding Yourself Out of the Body

During that initial experience with Soul Travel, Ann had walked into the kitchen and the bedroom to look around her apartment.

"Hey, this is great," she'd said.

Each step of the way she'd thought of what to do next. It took her a while in the dream state to think of chanting *Wah Z*, the spiritual name of the Inner Master. This name took her to a higher level. Though her intuition urged some new experiment, nothing at first came to mind. But then it occurred to her to sit on the couch and do a spiritual exercise in her dream.

The spiritual exercise took her out of her apartment, into the hallway. There she had met the Inner Master.

That was the first and last experiment she had ever tried.

Finally, Ann understood why the Master didn't come up to her in the dream state and say, "OK, we'll go off to a Wisdom Temple. I'll do everything for you; you don't have to do anything."

The Dream Master wanted her to use her own creativity and initiative.

Most often, someone fails at Soul Travel or dream travel because of a fear of death. Ann started to experiment and have the experience of Soul Travel under her own terms, so this fear began to vanish.

In the broadest sense, Soul Travel can be used in every aspect of daily life. It encompasses a lot more than mere travel outside the body. Soul Travel is the expansion of consciousness. It allows one to live each day with more awareness of the greater wisdom and understanding that comes by grace of ECK, the Holy Spirit.

Answer to a Prayer

Dreams, visions, and other experiences mean little in and of themselves.

Yet in the context of our spiritual life, they are signs of how much we are in accord with life. In fact, the whole point of life is to teach us how to come into agreement with the Voice of God, the Light and Sound. Many find the road to their inner worlds through the teachings of ECKANKAR.

Often, however, it takes a personal tragedy to drive us in search of the meaning of life.

Betty (name changed) was a mother, very close to her son; she found ECKANKAR after his death in a motorcycle mishap. Devastated by the loss, she was unable to find comfort in church. She would cry through the whole service. If she could but feel closer to God, then maybe He would help her understand why the accident had occurred.

More important, where was her son now? Was he OK?

Her prayers for help in understanding were endless.

Five months later, while at her lowest ebb, there came an experience that changed her life. She thought at first it was a dream, but it was in fact Soul Travel.

Betty awoke in vivid consciousness in the other worlds. A bespectacled woman with grey streaks in her dark hair met Betty, and they talked for a few minutes.

"Do you know my son?" Betty asked, giving his name.

"Of course I know him," said the other. "He lives right over there in that white house." The scene, a pastoral setting of cottages, looked like a lake resort.

There she found her son, and they had a long conversation. He assured her that his health was better than it had been on earth. Then he looked at her and said, "I know what you're doing to yourself. Please stop. You're hurting yourself."

Before they parted, she asked if she could hold him in her arms, since she didn't get a chance to do so before his death. Merry laughter twinkled in his eyes.

"OK, Mom," he said.

Soul Travel had brought her to him. She could still feel his warmth in her arms when she awoke. Even his scent lingered. A peaceful, happy feeling lasted for weeks before it began to fade. Betty became determined to learn all about her son's new home in heaven. Somewhere on earth, she knew, someone had the answer. That was the juncture where her sister introduced her to ECKANKAR.

The first book Betty read was *The Spiritual Notebook*, by Paul Twitchell. It convinced her that here was the answer to her prayers. Here was an explanation about the other worlds that made sense.

Grief for her son still overtakes Betty on

occasion. So she looks to the MAHANTA, the Living ECK Master to help her regain the tranquillity she felt while with her son during Soul Travel. She continues to do the Spiritual Exercises of ECK every day.

Some inner travel techniques are in the ECK dream discourses, which come with enrollment in ECKANKAR. More methods are in the book *The Spiritual Exercises of ECK*, available from ECKANKAR.

Betty now directs her efforts toward seeing the divine Light and hearing the holy Sound—keys to the secret worlds of God.

A story like this may inspire one to look for love and truth. Yet the actual finding depends upon doing the right thing. For those in ECK, it is doing the spiritual exercises, which are in many ECK books and discourses. They take a mere ten to twenty minutes a day. A chant, mantra, is simply a love song to God or a way to key in to the Divine Spirit. A chant helps you appreciate life.

Many ECKists adapt the Spiritual Exercises of ECK to dovetail with their own state of affairs once they catch the knack from the ECK teachings.

GAZING AT A BRIGHT OBJECT

This technique gets you out of the physical state into a higher consciousness. Just focus on a bright object like a coin, a diamond, a prism, or a crystal.

Gaze steadily at the object. Then imagine going out of your body by feeling light, happy, and full of love.

While thus concentrating, repeat this affirmation: "I am leaving my body. I want to see the Temple of ECK in Chanhassen, Minnesota."

Do this over and over until it becomes so.

You will find yourself outside the body, viewing it with joy and amazement. Look around for the MAHANTA. He is in the Temple sanctuary—a dear, old friend of yours.

Key First Meetings with ECK Masters

The mission of ECKANKAR is to show all the way home to God through Soul Travel and other means.

One's first meeting with the MAHANTA, the Living ECK Master may be quite ordinary, an occasion to excite little interest. The moment could slip by without any apparent significance. So the individual misses it, lost among the general conditions of the time and place it occurs.

On the other hand, a first meeting with the Master may have a dramatic impact. Such is the range of effects one may find when approaching the Master for the first time.

A woman from a Sun Belt state of the United States tells of the time she met Wah Z in a San Francisco hotel lobby. It was the mid-1950s. That was some twenty-five years before he took his place as the spiritual head of ECKANKAR.

A stranger had handed her a copy of *ECKANKAR—The Key to Secret Worlds*, by Paul Twitchell. But the book held nothing for her. True, parts of it did support her views on life, but overall she saw little value in it. The stranger had not revealed his identity. And soon, every trace of this incident washed from her conscious mind. It was years later before she recognized him.

Please note, *ECKANKAR—The Key to Secret Worlds* was first published in 1969, about fifteen years after she'd met the stranger in the hotel lobby.

Thirty years after that occasion, in the mid-1980s, she learned his name at an ECKANKAR meeting. His face was on a book jacket. Only then did she recognize today's Living ECK Master.

The man looked the same as she remembered him in the San Francisco hotel lobby way back in the 1950s. The memory of that meeting with the Spiritual Traveler rushed in.

It took years of spiritual preparation

before her Spiritual Eye opened.

How does her story fit in with Soul Travel? The trials of everyday life temper an individual to prepare for the Master. After this initial, often unheralded, meeting, a seeker begins a long course of training that leads to Soul Travel and the Master.

But little seems to change in everyday things.

Home to God

Soul Travel is simply the best means for Soul to go home to God. However, some who wish to master it have lesser ideals. They want to learn this ancient science for healing. Others see it as a way to make a fortune, spy on people, steal business secrets, get attention as crime solvers, or earn a living as specialists in lost-and-found items. They harbor every motive except a desire for God.

After an individual first meets the MAHANTA, the Master employs the dream state to prepare him for the Light and Sound of God.

Glen, let's say, is an initiate who did a spiritual exercise to reach a certain plane in contemplation. The Inner Master obliged him. The Master lifted him into the far worlds. There, he drove Glen by car through a residential neighborhood at night. The houses rolled by. All at once, the brightest light you could imagine blazed from an empty lot. Its blinding flash was like a magnesium flare.

But the MAHANTA knew the pure Light of God could destroy Glen due to his spiritual impurities. So the Master sped by the Light. This quick action prevented injury to Glen's sensitive Spiritual Eye.

At the outset of this experience, Glen had heard the Sound of that plane. It carried him deep into the Far Country. Yet he knew that it takes Light, Sound, and the Master for a full spiritual consummation. The Inner Master had met him. The Sound had lifted him to that high plane. Yet where was the Light? It was necessary to show the way through the dark.

Soul Travel is the line of action that

Soul takes on Its final journey home to God. In other words, Soul Travel is Soul's return to Its place of origin.

Home.

* * *

Monica learns that love conquers death. Her story first appeared in Earth to God, Come In Please..., *book 1.*

Dad's Gift from the Other Side

By Monica Wylie

I was about fifteen when my father died of a heart attack. He'd been born with a heart problem. Growing up, I sometimes felt responsible for my father's painful angina. He wanted to do things with me, but my pace was too fast.

One day while at school, I had a sudden knowingness that my father was about to leave us. I saw him inwardly as he read an ECKANKAR book.

He said, "I want to rest."

Then in my inner vision, he laid down the book in his lap and translated (passed on) to a higher plane of existence. Sensing my family's concern as it reached out to me at school, I couldn't concentrate in class. Later at home that day, everybody was peering out the window, waiting for me. My mom opened the door.

When I saw her, I knew.

I took my dad's passing badly because I missed him. I missed the hugging and holding, his touch and kindly voice, but because I had grown up with Spirit, the ECK, I wasn't angry. Inside, I knew that his death was simply a translation to a new life for him.

That night, though, I was afraid to go to bed. I'd never been afraid like this before! I wanted to sleep with my mom, but she wanted to be alone. When I got in my bed I felt my father's presence in the room, so I clutched the sheets up to my eyes, ready to cover my head.

Suddenly Dad appeared. He had his white sweater and glasses on, as though he were physically there. As he walked toward my bed, I felt scared—though I sensed he didn't want to scare me.

I felt Dad's gentle voice. "Don't be scared, Monica," he said.

My first reaction was to jump under the covers. As a child, I sometimes saw ghosts in my room, so covering my head with the blankets was an old habit. But after a moment, I pulled the sheet down. Dad was still there. I remember apologizing for being so scared.

"Don't be scared," he said again. "You know better, now that you've been in ECK for so long."

He came closer. As he walked by my foot, he gave it an affectionate slap. "I love you," he said. His strong fingers hit my foot, just as he'd always done in the morning to wake me up.

Then the vision faded. This visit was Dad's signal that he was off to say goodbye to a few other people.

A friend of my father verified my experience. He'd felt a slap on his back. When he turned around saying, "What the heck was that?" he saw my father. Dad used these familiar touches to let people know he was all right.

I dreamed about Dad too. One night he came to take me dancing.

"No, Dad," I said, "I would rather watch."

As I looked on, he danced with several nondescript beings. I felt his joy at being able to dance, finally free from the pain of angina.

As time went on, we watched each other grow. It wasn't important to my father how I grew up physically, only how I grew spiritually. Dad would drive up in his blue car during a dream or spiritual exercise, and we would visit different heavenly planes. He'd take me to see this scene or that sight in the inner worlds. Sometimes it was to a park.

At our destination, the Inner Master, the MAHANTA, would teach us from my father's ECK discourses. We thus progressed through the Astral and Mental Planes.

Now I visit him on the Etheric Plane. He doesn't wear glasses anymore, and he appears thinner and much finer. That's closer to the real him. You see, as he gets higher, I see him more as pure Soul.

One day he said, "I'm not your father anymore; remember that. I only worked as your father on the physical plane. But always remember, the love of being your father is still there. I love you, and you love me, and that's how it is now."

I can't wait to pass this love on to my children.

This Soul keeps teaching me, a gift for which I'm very grateful to the Inner Master. The man who was my father is a Coworker with God now—that's his true occupation. He's in the inner worlds, though he's also in my heart.

And someday, I'll be a Coworker with God just like him.

3
Beyond Soul Travel: Seeing, Knowing, and Being

Soul Travel is simply Soul's movement to God.

This practice is what many devotees of world religions have sought in vain in their own teachings. Soul Travel is an active method of going home to God. The term itself is a dynamic way to express this natural means of ascending to the pinnacle of heaven or plumbing the depths of God's love for Its creation.

Soul Travel is also a cleansing agent for Soul.

Rather than expect you to grasp a full understanding of the philosophy behind Soul Travel, I give stories and examples to tell of its workings. In time, with your own experience as a gauge, you will know what's most important here. The words on these pages are like flower seeds planted in the fertile soil of your heart. You'll remember all you need to, when you need to, for taking a new step toward the infinite love and mercy of God.

Everything has a time and season. So be patient.

Stories are important, because they paint a watercolor for our minds. Like seeds or little time capsules, they burst upon the mind's canvas and add a rich dimension to our recall. So when you need to remember a certain spiritual point, the right story will come to mind. A story can satisfy spiritual hunger in a way that logic cannot.

Soul Travel and the expansion of consciousness make us aware of the effect of our words and actions upon others, and ultimately, upon ourselves.

We make our own heaven and hell.

Soul Travel via Imagination

A gentleman once told how as a boy he loved to attend mass. In church, he sat among the other worshippers and marveled at the statues of saints that towered over the congregation on high pedestals. Some statues reached near the ceiling.

How wonderful it would be to stand beside them, he thought.

So, while others bent their heads in prayer, this industrious lad did Soul Travel. In the Soul body, he rose above his human body and stationed himself next to the saints, whose heads soared to such heights.

One day, he shared his unique ability with his mother. He confessed how he loved the wonderful experience of rising up near the ceiling by the statues. Why, he could leave his pew and fly up among the saints. Even better, no one could see him. His mother pursed her lips, trying to be clear in her mind on where her son claimed to go.

"You mean in front of the altar?" she asked.

"No," he said. "I mean up there by the ceiling."

"Don't speak such foolishness," she said.

That was that. The boy was still and said no more. Yet he wondered about his mother's reaction to what he had revealed. A frosty ear, indeed.

He had seen and felt himself in another location, in more than his imagination. No doubt about it. For where imagination is, there is Soul. It surprised him to find that others who went to mass never left their pews in their subtle bodies to float around in church. How dull.

What's the point in going to church? he wondered.

I tell this story to show that you too can move into the hidden worlds beyond our physical one. It all starts with the imagination. But first, fear and guilt must go. They are like the bricks and mortar of a high stone wall that separates us from our true spiritual rights.

They lock out freedom.

Conscious Soul Travel

Our first visits to the inner planes are often in the dream state. On occasion, a few people have the good fortune to begin with Soul Travel, sometimes even before contact with the outer works of ECK.

Earl, let's call him, wrote about a Soul Travel experience of some years ago. It was long before he'd heard of ECKANKAR or the Spiritual Travelers of ECK.

Earl was then a soldier stationed at a military base. Asleep in the barracks at night, he was often baffled to find himself out of the body, walking through walls. Still, he thought it a fantastic adventure.

There were also other times when he left his body. However, his out-of-body travel all took place in the barracks, with no ranging abroad. Yet this ability lent him the unique faculty of seeing through walls and lockers, where he could scan stored clothing and the personal effects of other GIs.

He felt like a man with X-ray vision.

But despite all these early out-of-body experiences, Earl made a curious discovery. He did not Soul Travel after his Second Initiation in ECK. He now describes his state of spiritual consciousness as one in which "I see, I know, I am."

Seeing, Knowing, and Being.

He speaks of the "I" consciousness which exists on the Soul Plane. Soul Travel is a quick way to move into the higher worlds, but once an individual becomes an inhabitant of the Soul Plane, there is no sense of movement. Perceptions are immediate and direct.

Though all may begin the path of ECK with dreams and then move on to Soul

Travel, the day comes when Soul Travel changes to a new method of gaining experience.

Then comes a high state of consciousness—direct perception. It lets us gain experience by the simple mode of Seeing, Knowing, and Being. This change marks one's acceptance as a citizen of the first of the spiritual worlds.

That is the Soul Plane.

The Secret Path to Heaven

The ECK teachings mark the secret path to heaven. The ECK books and discourses brought this spiritual path to light. So, do the Spiritual Exercises of ECK and stretch your creative powers. Try a certain technique for a couple of weeks or months to see a spiritual breakthrough. Yes, it may take a while. The human consciousness needs time to adjust so it can receive the enlightenment of God in full measure when it's due. Even without a visual experience of the Blue Light or the Inner Master, you enjoy a divine knowingness. You know that your spiritual life is in good hands.

You just know.

All need not pass through the stage of having to study the introductory ECK works before earning a right to Soul Travel. For some it comes sooner. Past-life training in the spiritual works also comes into play. It affords what appears to be a shortcut to others, who must run the entire course to develop a firm spiritual foundation.

Soul Travel takes you through the psychic worlds. These are the worlds of matter, energy, space, and time. So it stands to reason, within the limits of time, that if you wish to travel, there is distance—space—between here and there. Distance is a separation in time. So it's going to take a certain amount of time to travel from here to there.

In the worlds below the Soul Plane, this concept of time and space is basic science.

However, in the spiritual God Worlds of ECK, from the Soul Plane on up, there is no space as we think of it. Nor is there time. Both are collapsed; they do not exist. So what need is there for Soul Travel?

Soul Travel will carry you only so far, to the Soul Plane, but then you begin to discover the high states of Seeing, Knowing, and Being.

It is there that the real adventure begins.

Moving Past Soul Travel

After you learn Soul Travel, a time comes to give it up. It is merely a part of your spiritual evolution.

Those in ECK who show a measure of progress will reach the Soul Plane, a kingdom beyond time and space. It means there is no movement of anything, including Soul. So when you move above the Mental Plane to the Soul Plane, you no longer Soul Travel. It's impossible. There, you develop the skill of Seeing, Knowing, and Being. Instead of movement, therefore, you reach another plane of spiritual consciousness within an instant.

You are simply there.

The Ancient Science of Soul Travel is needed to bridge the gap from the Physical Plane to the Soul Plane.

Some Soul Travel experiences are sensational events. Yet the whole idea of the Inner Master taking you on a Soul Travel journey is to give you a life-sustaining experience needed for spiritual maturity. With it, he proves survival beyond death. Without the Master's help, you will ride the wheel of karma and reincarnation to the end of time.

Thanks to ECK, however, there is a better way.

There is the Traveler, the Inner Master.

* * *

Doug tells of an unexpected visit to loved ones. From Earth to God, Come In Please..., *book 2.*

Soul Travel Surprise

By Doug Munson

I sat with my sister, her boyfriend, and about forty other people in an ECKANKAR workshop on past lives, dreams, and Soul Travel.

Thrilled as I was to be with my sister after an absence of a few years, I still felt an empty spot. I missed my wife, April, and our two boys. They couldn't make the trip to the ECK Worldwide Seminar with me.

At about two in the afternoon, the facilitators asked our group to try a Soul Travel exercise.

"Place your attention above and between your eyebrows," they said.

This point is the Tisra Til, or the Third Eye. It's a place where Soul—you, as a conscious, individual spark of God—resides.

"Now take a deep breath, and join us in singing *HU*. It's pronounced like the word *hue*. HU is an ancient name for God; it's sung as a love song to God. Now imagine a place you would like to be right now, just for a moment or two."

I knew where that was—home.

Together our group sang *HU*. The sound filled the room like a celestial symphony. It spirited me to Minneapolis, to the couch in our living room where I sat for a second with my hands folded. Then I got up, moved around, and looked in on the boys playing. April was busy with household chores. Although it all seemed to be just my imagination, it still felt real. It felt warm and comfortable to be with them.

But then the facilitators recalled us from the Soul Travel exercise to the workshop. My sister and her friend said they had enjoyed their experiences too.

Then it was off to other meetings.

We three met the next morning to hear Sri Harold Klemp speak. Later, my sister and her friend treated me to a walk along the beach and a quick tour of Hollywood before they drove me to the airport for my afternoon flight home to Minneapolis.

That evening my family greeted me at the airport with hugs and animated stories about the week we'd spent apart. On the ride home I told April all about my sister and that her friend was a nice guy. But I wanted April and the boys to know how much I'd missed them, so I told of the Soul Travel workshop.

"I Soul Traveled home Saturday," I said.

Wide-eyed, April looked at me and said, "What time was that?"

"Oh, a little after two, California time."

"You know," she said, pointing to my younger son, "around four o'clock our time, this little guy said, 'Mommy, I just saw Dad in the kitchen with you out of the corner of my eye. He was standing next to you with his hand on your shoulder.'"

Allowing for the difference in time zones, it was the exact same time.

4
The Light and Sound of God

An old misunderstanding about Soul Travel is that it is nothing more than a simple occult projection out of the body, into the Astral Plane. Yet Soul Travel is an all-inclusive skill. It goes well beyond the Astral Plane and into the Causal, Mental, and Etheric Planes. Then, right on to the Soul Plane.

Soul Travel is thus a modern way to speak of Soul on Its journey home to God.

Several phases one may expect in ECK include dreams, visions, Soul Travel, the

ECKshar consciousness, and God Consciousness. Each of these facets reflects a magnification of God's Light and Sound for the traveler.

Each phase of spiritual attainment in ECK offers a set of experiences, and each phase leads to a higher plane.

A vision, to cite an example, is a pre–Soul Travel event. An individual, still bound to the physical body, hangs back from admitting to an all-out search for God. All the more so if it means leaving the security of the human shell. So the light of truth slips in upon him with a vision. A vision is a promising start toward the Kingdom of God.

Our goal is God-Realization in this lifetime.

There's More

An example of a vision is this report from a doctor in California.

In contemplation, he relaxed and declared he was a channel for the MAHANTA, the SUGMAD (God), and Sat Nam (mighty ruler of the Fifth, or Soul, Plane). He was ready to quit his contemplative session after a bit as no results were in sight. Then, in his Spiritual Eye, a flood of colored rays beamed from heaven and into him. The different colors, he judged, stood for the MAHANTA, the SUGMAD, and Sat Nam.

Then a voice said, "That's not all there is."

A strong impression told him that a missing part of his declaration at the start of contemplation was the all-important ECK, the Holy Spirit of God. So he now declared himself also a vehicle for the ECK, and thereupon the heavens filled with the Light and Sound of God.

"A wonderful experience," he said.

If one has a vision of this kind, he is beginning to see the deeper secrets beyond the reach of the human eye.

A REMINDER

If you wish to Soul Travel at night while your body sleeps, remind yourself of this desire a few times during the day. For example, tell yourself, *Tonight I will Soul Travel in my dream.*

Your mind will better accept an idea if it's repeated throughout the day.

Now visualize the sort of dream you would like. Make believe it's real. Picture the dream, picture its results. You may also play a movie scene in your mind of the advice or help you seek from the Dream Master.

Dreams Lead to Soul Travel

The dream is a natural, early phase of training that the MAHANTA, the Living ECK Master employs to instruct a student.

Soon the individual finds the makeup of his dreams changing from pre-ECK days. The fogginess, the pointlessness, of dreams begins to clear. The sunlight of truth now beams in. So one senses a new direction in his inner worlds; it brings into being dreams of clarity and meaning. The dream state is thus a basic part of the MAHANTA's teaching. To be sure, there are no clear-cut boundaries to mark out the multiple levels of experience.

So an ECKist, one far along in initiations, may report what, on the face of it, appear to be ordinary dreams or run-of-the-mill visions.

As a rule, though, this is seldom the case. He's moved on. The closer an initiate of ECK comes to God, the more he lives and moves in full consciousness. A unique state of awareness is his signature in every world he enters.

Dreams and visions are a fascinating subject. Yet an ECKist finds that Soul Travel probes a lot deeper into the riddle of life than do any astral or mental projections.

Hence his goal is total awareness, and he puts away the toys of psychic phenomena.

Visiting Inner Worlds

The next example shows a two-part play of ECK: giving and receiving. It starts with a dream and moves on to Soul Travel.

In a dream, then, the MAHANTA handed an ECK dreamer a photograph of the dreamer with two young men. All stood next to a lamppost. The dreamer handed them something. When he awoke, the meaning of the dream was clear: He was giving light to these two individuals, as shown by the lamppost.

The dream's images left no doubt.

Yet this dream led to a second occurrence. To better understand his dream, this ECKist went into contemplation but soon fell asleep.

He awoke in Sat Lok, the Soul Plane. This was more than a commonplace dream. This experience was an actual visit to the dividing line between the material worlds and the spiritual planes. Rebazar Tarzs met him there. This wonderful ECK Master had taken a special interest in him, showing him the way to spiritual maturity. Rebazar told this devotee that he'd now gained enough understanding to teach ECK to others.

The message was for the dreamer to get into the mainstream of life.

The dream experience by the lamppost had led to a visit to the Soul Plane. Notice, there is no sharp line of demarcation between the dream phase and the Soul Travel experience that followed. For Soul Travel was indeed the second part of this event.

All in all, visions and dreams lead the way to Soul Travel, though it's no fixed rule.

This crossing from dreams to Soul Travel is a major development in our spiritual lives. It marks a conscious effort to travel into the far worlds of God, a desire in line with the aim of Soul.

Our mission is to become a Coworker with SUGMAD, the God of all. Thereby we gain an ever-greater love for and awareness of the Creator, Its creation, and every creature within it.

Soul Travel is thus the most direct way to see the heavenly worlds inside us.

Light and Sound

Yes, for the most part, Soul Travel is a function of the lower worlds of matter, energy, space, and time. Yet it is the most direct way to pass through the material worlds to the spiritual realms above. So it is a valuable tool.

Almost anyone can learn it. All it takes is an earnest desire and the drive to realize the Kingdom of God here and now, in this very lifetime.

Soul Travel is therefore a bridge. It arches over the gulf that keeps the human from the divine. It is a natural but unrecognized talent that develops with the Spiritual Exercises of ECK.

Here follows an example of how Soul Travel may lead to a higher spiritual state.

A chela in Africa lay down in bed, covered his ears with pillows, then listened for the Sound of ECK. Listening for this holy

Sound is very much a spiritual exercise. Like a sweet, though rushing wind off in the distance, this divine melody seemed at once both near and far. In fact, it was inside him. Soon came the sensation of a gentle tugging at the top of his head. He stayed calm. Then came a total liberation from his human shell.

In the magnificent Soul body, surrounded by love and goodwill, he hovered over his human form in bed with wonder.

"The whole of this space was lighted with shimmering atoms and bright giant and small stars," he said.

He studied his appearance. To his great joy, he found the radiant Soul body alive with energy and power.

Now he sang *SUGMAD* in a gentle lullaby. Thereupon he knew that all the glittering atoms and stars were a part of him. As he sang, energy began to vibrate from inside him, flowing out to sustain all things and beings in this unending universe of stars. What tremendous love and mercy he felt for all beings in this expanse of light!

A great Sound now arose from his breast. It touched and granted bliss, life, and power to all in his worlds. That, in turn, lifted him into a spiritual ecstasy, due to his act of giving love and mercy to all.

Now and again the ecstasy returns.

The experience was one of brief homage to the SUGMAD (God). It still enriches his life in every way. This experience began as Soul Travel. Indeed, it went far beyond, turning into a spiritual journey to the high worlds of God. And yet, the hem of God's garment is not the whole of it.

If the full God experience came to one without preparation, it would cause a setback of long duration.

Leaving the Body

A classic Soul Travel experience sees one leave the human body in full awareness, with the Light and Sound of God streaming into the Soul body.

Some people have done that in an earlier life and need not learn the ABCs of

Soul Travel. But the MAHANTA gives them a brushup course. It acts like a springboard to the holy states of Seeing, Knowing, and Being. To see, know, and be are qualities of Soul at the foreground of our attention on the Soul Plane and higher.

These three attributes are the fruit of the ECKshar consciousness.

Soul Travel thus starts with one's state of consciousness today. It takes the human consciousness and stretches it, giving a person a new, deeper insight into the wonder and complexity of creation.

Now let's look at a striking, but rare sort of Soul Travel. It shows how this ancient science blends into the affairs and circumstances of each seeker's makeup.

Michael from Ghana once had an experience that shook his beliefs about physical reality. The experience raised some questions. Those concerns led him, in the several years to come, on a search for answers.

Michael has a practical mind, albeit a very complex one. So an ECK Master sent him on a unique out-of-body trip to challenge and expand his understanding.

Michael had heard and read about people in Ghana, non-ECKists, who'd become lost in strange, invisible, and mysterious towns that they claimed did not exist. Their experiences confounded them. After they told their tales, it was next to impossible to believe them. Moreover, there were also stories of people who'd died but were reported in encounters in other parts of Ghana. Sometimes these "dead" people vanished into thin air when a living person confronted them.

But none of that was on Michael's mind on that ordinary day as he set out on some personal errands in the city of Accra.

A taxi dropped him off at his first stop without incident. His business in the government office lasted ten minutes. The next stop was a short distance away, along a tree-shaded street, so Michael decided to walk. From there, errands done, he took a fancy to walk home.

That is where he entered a twilight zone.

A tall, stout man of thirty-five called to him from behind. "Do you know the location of the Ministry of Education Annex?"

Michael said no. They parted ways.

Five minutes later Michael was lost. He thought he knew the streets of Accra like his hand, but the unfamiliar streets and buildings around him were a labyrinth of confusion. What was going on? Michael asked directions. He followed one through a narrow lane set between a house and a mansion.

His position was hopeless. What part of Accra could this be?

The experience ran on, taking him outside the city to a suburb. But that town lay in the wrong direction. Petrol (service) stations, churches, the city's traffic circle—all familiar locations—were either gone or changed in appearance.

Poor Michael. To say he was in a confused state is to make light of his misfortune.

Nor could he retrace his steps. Streets were new or laid out in a different way. Worse, the service station of a few minutes ago had vanished, as had a beer bar with a blue canopy over the door. Michael only broke free of this experience after he caught a regular city bus from that suburb to Accra.

Later, he could not duplicate the route of his strange journey into an even stranger dimension.

Of course, it perplexed him.

He'd never read of anything like it in the ECK teachings, but he drew a few conclusions on his own. First, was it possible that this physical plane had many levels that are kept separate from each other by different vibrations? Can such exist side by side, invisible to each other?

Yes, it's true. No absolute line of demarcation separates the Physical Plane from the Astral Plane, so the very top vibrations of the physical world blend into the lower astral region beyond.

Then crossover visits occur.

Second, the question, When did he enter the invisible world?

He concluded that it all began when

the tall, stout stranger called to him from behind. (That stranger was an ECK Master. He'd come to help Michael expand his state of consciousness in a manner that fit Michael's state of awareness.)

To sum up, this otherworldly experience began with the stranger and ended with Michael on a bus back to familiar grounds in Accra.

Of interest here is that Michael could not escape this strange morass of events without the impartial aid of a bus driver. To be sure, this was an uncommon Soul Travel experience. Yet it taught Michael that the stories he'd heard about strange towns and people in Ghana were true. A Westerner might have a good laugh at such a tale, but the people of Ghana know better.

And so does Michael.

Beginners in Soul Travel like to stay close to the body. It gives them confidence. So the MAHANTA or another ECK Master will help them shed the human state of consciousness and stick to a short journey into a higher plane.

An experience like this may include a feeling of moving out of the body, of floating through a ceiling or wall, or even of flying into space.

A glimmer of light shines at the remote edge of this space. The Spiritual Traveler guides the novice toward it, and they emerge into a most novel setting. There an intriguing world beguiles the newcomer.

The new Soul Traveler may there explore city streets that are much like those on earth. The people, however, go about duties unknown to earth.

For example, some of them greet arrivals who have died on the Physical Plane to resume spiritual lessons on the Astral. Others guide Souls who visit the Astral Plane during dreams. Whatever duties the Astral Plane dwellers perform, they all serve the spiritual hierarchy in many vital ways that make life go around, as do people in every part of God's vast kingdom.

Riding the Wave Home

Soul Travel is a very enriching part of ECKANKAR. Its main benefit is to let us tap into the wisdom and knowledge we've gained in the other worlds. Thus we may enjoy a heightened state of awareness twenty-four hours a day.

It is in this way that the inner and outer experiences build upon each other, to bring more love, joy, and understanding into our lives. This deep insight into the workings of everyday life is more important than any single experience out of the body.

However, Soul Travel incorporates many experiences from the inner worlds and weaves them into a tapestry of exquisite beauty and value beyond price.

That is Soul Travel.

In ECKANKAR, we turn aside from false authority. We acknowledge only the real guidance that rises from the heart. The power to do so comes from the MAHANTA, the Living ECK Master. If you meet with a Soul Travel or out-of-the-body experience, don't ask someone else to validate it. You are the sole judge. Prove your own experience. You alone must determine its value.

Beyond its exciting side, Soul Travel is a direct way to hear the Sound and see the Light of God. That cannot be done from the human consciousness. The Sound and Light are the wave of divine love that Soul catches into the kingdom of heaven; they are the twin aspects of the ECK, the Holy Spirit.

The ECK is the Voice of God, the Comforter, the spirit of truth.

By the time one learns the secrets of visions, dreams, Soul Travel, and the ECK-shar consciousness, he is an experienced traveler in the high regions of God.

Then comes the crown of realization, the enlightenment of God.

Experience is our hallmark in ECK. An individual may read all the books on faith and spirituality in a metropolitan library, but reading nets him nothing in the God Worlds. Only experience goes beyond the detours and dead ends of life. Only experience reveals the correct road to the realm of the All.

So a milestone in Soul's supreme journey to God is the art and science of Soul Travel.

A GATEWAY TO SOUL TRAVEL

If you want to learn Soul Travel, do this technique tonight. Before sleep, shut your eyes and place your attention on the Spiritual Eye. It's right above and between the eyebrows.

Then sing *HU*. Fill your heart, mind, and body with warm love.

This feeling of love grants the confidence to venture into some new, unexplored area of your spiritual being. A way to fill yourself with love is to call up a warm, comfy memory, like a child's hug or a mate's kiss.

Just so the feeling warms your heart with deep love.

Now, eyes still shut, look into the Spiritual Eye for the holy person who is your ideal, whether Christ or an ECK

Master. In a gentle voice say, "I give you permission to take me to the best place for my spiritual good."

Then chant *HU*, *God*, or some other holy word.

Next, see yourself in a familiar place, like a special room in your home. Be assured that the guide who comes is a dear, long-standing friend.

Do this session five or six times over as many days.

A spiritual exercise is like a physical exercise in that all muscles need time to respond. So, do this spiritual exercise at least a week before you consider throwing in the towel. Success comes with diligence. And if you do an exercise routine for a couple of weeks, you may surprise yourself at your new spiritual outlook.

Thus, the same kind of discipline applies to both physical and spiritual exercises.

The sole purpose of the Spiritual Exercises of ECK is to open a conduit, or channel, between you and the Holy Spirit, the Audible Life Stream. The origin of this wave is the heart of God. The moment you begin to sing *HU* and look for truth in this particular way, changes of a positive nature do awaken within you.

You may not see them at first, but your friends and family will.

* * *

Death has a long arm, as Rhonda saw, but the reach of life is longer still. This story is from Earth to God, Come In Please..., *book 2.*

A Death That Changed My Life

By Rhonda Mattern

In 1986, I married a French ECKist. I remember thinking how bizarre, yet wonderful it was to spend my entire wedding reception seated in a corner with my new mother-in-law. We discussed ECKANKAR in French.

My mother-in-law, whom I'll call

Sophie, felt alarm over her son's involvement in ECKANKAR. During our conversation, she interrogated me about each wedding guest.

"That man over there in the nice suit. Is he in ECKANKAR?"

"Oui, Sophie."

"And the woman from Togo; I hear she's a lawyer. Is she involved in this too?"

"Oui, Sophie."

"And the doctor from Versailles? He's in ECK?"

"Oui, Sophie."

She was incredulous. How could all these normal people be involved in something she thought so strange?

Over the next several years, Sophie and I had many heart-to-heart talks about ECK and other subjects. She even read an ECK book or two, and though she became more comfortable with ECKANKAR, she remained a skeptic.

My husband and I divorced in 1992 but remained good friends. I stayed in touch with his parents, planning to visit them after the 1992 ECKANKAR European Seminar.

A few weeks before my trip to Europe, I got an urgent call from my ex-husband. My heart raced as I tried to make sense of his news: His mother, Sophie, had committed suicide. My mind rushed in five hundred directions at once. Sophie, vibrant and beautiful. Sophie, the woman with everything—the right car, the right husband, the right house on the French Riviera, the right clothes.

I hung up the phone in a daze. For hours I paced from one end of my apartment to the other, crying uncontrollably. Somehow it was hard to accept the fact I would never see her again.

"Wait a minute!" I said. "I *can* see her again!"

Conscious Soul Travel had never been my strong point. Although my years in ECKANKAR brought many incredible out-of-body experiences and lucid dreams, I can rarely bring them on at will. However, in this moment of despair, I felt a new determination to brave the inner planes and see Sophie one last time.

I lay down on my bed and sang *HU* for a few minutes. Try as I might, nothing happened. I felt ashamed that after eighteen years in ECKANKAR, I still hadn't mastered the art of Soul Travel.

Once again, waves of sadness and loss washed over me, emotions that my mind labeled as negative. As I tried to push back these negative feelings, my mind drifted to a passage in one of Paul Twitchell's early books on ECKANKAR. In it, Paul finally succeeds in initiating a meeting with his teacher, the ECK Master Rebazar Tarzs. The secret, Paul found, was to travel on a vibrational field on the inner planes between himself and his teacher.

With a start I realized that the key was not putting aside my feelings, but using them as a way to travel to Sophie.

My feelings were beautiful, deep,

and totally fitting for the moment. They were a wave issuing from my heart, a wave to ride into the higher worlds.

With this in mind, I began to focus on my love for Sophie. I felt myself lifted in a dizzying, spiraling motion. Before long I stood on a cloud, with a confused-looking Sophie beside me.

A cloud, I thought.

How corny. This can't be real. Where are the temples, the Masters? This is just imagination.

Sophie was astonished to see me. She spoke to me in excited French.

"Rhonda, it's you! Am I still alive?"

"No. Well, *yes.* I mean, you died, but as Soul you're still alive."

"Why are you here? Are you dead too?"

"No, I wanted to visit you."

"So this ECKANKAR, it's all true, then?"

"Oui, Sophie."

In the conversation that followed, Sophie and I discussed the guilt she felt on committing suicide. The whole time I was talking to Sophie, part of me stood back, taking a critical look at this experience.

This can't be happening, I thought. *I must be making it up. I don't really have the ability to consciously Soul Travel.*

Suddenly, Wah Z (the spiritual name of Sri Harold Klemp) was by our side, glowing in a blaze of white light. I told Sophie I would like to introduce her to someone very special. She saw Wah Z and said, "Oh, it's the head of ECKANKAR. C'est la grosse légume [the big vegetable]."

This struck me as a funny comment, but so much was happening that I simply brushed it aside.

The three of us stood in a circle and hugged. I could hear sounds swirling around us and felt a love that words cannot tell. I wanted to stay in that moment forever, but try as I might, I couldn't hold on to the experience.

Suddenly I was back in my bedroom.

Rooted once more in the physical world, I started to doubt my experience. Each time a doubt would crop up, I'd hear the words *la grosse légume.* After a number of rounds of this, it occurred to me that a message from Divine Spirit was trying to get through.

I called a French friend. "Is *la grosse légume* a standard expression in French?" I asked.

He explained that "the big vegetable" was the equivalent of "the big cheese" in English. That made sense: Sophie loved to joke and tease. I could picture her seeing the MAHANTA for the first time and referring to him as "the big cheese of ECKANKAR."

Suddenly I froze. Wait a minute. I didn't know that expression in French. But Sophie did. That meant she *was* there.

My experience must have been real!

As the weeks and months pass, my mind still questions: Maybe I heard *la grosse légume* in conversation once and filed it away unconsciously. Maybe it was in a book. Maybe I knew it once but forgot it.

But as Soul, I know the truth. Last month, once again, I rode the waves of love to visit a dear friend on the inner planes.

5
Spiritual Exercises for Soul Travel

Whether Soul Travel fits one's spiritual needs is his business. If his heart says yes and he wants help, that's mine. I'm here to help.

Our Inborn Desire for God

Soul Travel puts zest into life. It is the most direct way to ease the spirit of yearning for God planted in every heart at birth.

"Seek God," says the heart.

Each awakening Soul is like the seeker in *Stranger by the River*. Listen to author Paul Twitchell:

"Outwardly, [the seeker's] life was little different from that of other people—working, toiling, laboring—yet his struggle to find life was deeper and more acute; the pain was greater, the suffering unbearable, and his sensitivity more intense.

"Nothing could lift him spiritually, and the responsibility or success which other men had would not touch him. He was the outcast, the lonely, and the dejected, for love had passed him by as there was nothing in his life which love had to anchor upon."

Then a beam of grace lit the seeker. He met the Spiritual Traveler. And with the Master came divine love.

If the seeker's quest rings a bell in you, try the following exercise, The Easy Way.

THE EASY WAY

Just before sleep, place attention upon your Spiritual Eye. It is between the eyebrows. Then sing *HU* or *God* silently.

Fix attention on a blank movie screen in your inner vision, and keep it free of any pictures. If unwanted mental thoughts, images, or pictures do flash up on the screen of your imagination, replace them with the face of the Living ECK Master.

After a few minutes of silence, you may hear a faint clicking sound in one ear, perhaps like the sound of a cork popping from a bottle. You will find yourself in the Soul form in a most natural way, looking back at your physical body in bed.

Now, would you like to go on a short outing?

There is nothing to fear, for no harm can come to you while outside the body. The MAHANTA will be with you to keep watch over your progress and offer support. After a while, the Soul body will return and slide gently into the physical self.

That is all there is to it.

97

If this exercise is not successful the first time, try it again later. The technique works. It has worked for many others.

What Is Soul Travel?

"Soul Travel is an individual experience, a realization of survival," says *The Shariyat-Ki-SUGMAD, Books One & Two*. "It is an inner experience through which comes beauty and love of all life. It cannot be experienced in rituals and ceremonies, nor bottled in creeds."

Realization means to be fully aware of something.

Proof of Soul's survival comes every time a person goes to sleep. Sleep is an out-of-body experience. Few realize that. Proof of Soul's survival is in the awakening, and thus sleep may be called "the little death." During sleep, Soul leaves the physical body and travels to some other place. It then returns, and the body awakens.

Yet to the average person, this natural process of Soul's comings and goings is an unconscious act. The enlightened ones, however, are in full control of the process.

Realization, like experience, is an individual matter.

Much misunderstanding and fear exist about a God-given ability like Soul Travel. To protect itself from the insecurity of the unknown, the public girds itself in fear. It weaves a web of hostility to contain the unknown and so tries to isolate itself with a net of superstitions.

The average man on the street treats the unknown with more than a trace of suspicion.

Realization, at its core, is the other side of ignorance. Realization parts the curtain that separates truth from lie, fact from fiction, and the known from the unknown. The curtain is of the Kal's manufacture. The Kal Niranjan is the king of negativity, and his job is to keep all Souls in ignorance. He hides from them their everlasting nature.

Soul, the ever awakened, exists beyond the sleep state of the human consciousness.

To take a new viewpoint about something brings understanding about the little things of life. For example, a woman wrote to say that Soul Travel was, in one instance, a very subtle experience for her. Yet the outcome produced a major shift in consciousness for her.

Note the practicality of Soul Travel in the following story.

She tells of her parents well along in years. Both are in their nineties. For fifteen years, she went to their home once a week for lunch or dinner—to keep an eye on them and stay in touch. It occurred to her how much she'd learned from them over the years.

One week, the three had a talk about elders and the day they're unable to care for themselves. Wouldn't their children, with the best of intentions, invite them to come live with them or move closer?

Her parents gave their view of this seemingly generous offer.

They would not want to move. If they did, everything would be new, and they wouldn't know anyone. They'd have to start over. A move meant a new church, new doctors, new friends—a high-stress change for younger couples in good health. But they, with far less energy than the young, would meet too much stress for comfort.

The daughter, of course, got the point. She could see how her well-meaning intentions would look from her parents' side of the curtain. So she left well enough alone. She respected their wishes to stay in their present home.

A clear realization, it was nonetheless a far-from-dramatic kind of Soul Travel.

Soul Travel means moving into a new, higher state of consciousness. Its result is always of positive effect. By sprinkling light on darkness, Soul Travel brings love, wisdom, and freedom to all it touches.

Soul Travel, therefore, is a means of changing an old viewpoint to a new, higher one.

If you want a down-to-earth exercise of Soul Travel, you'll like the next one. Stick with it. Then watch your state of awareness stretch and grow into one of a greater love and appreciation, for you'll find the spiritual treasures already within your grasp.

It'll be your little secret.

AROUND THE ROOM

This spiritual exercise uses the imaginative body.

Take a seat in a chair in your kitchen. Make yourself comfortable. Then say, "I shall go for a short walk in the Soul body."

Shut your eyes. Look into the Spiritual Eye in a soft, sweet, gentle way. Sing *HU* for a minute or two. Now, in your imagination, see and feel yourself stand up from the chair.

If I were to do this contemplation, I would say, "I shall rise from the chair in my Soul body and walk around the kitchen table."

Then I'd study the kitchen, the color and pattern of the tablecloth, and the flowers in a vase. Also, the fruit bowl on the counter, and the breadbox.

While the physical body continues in contemplation with eyes shut, I'd walk to the window in the imaginative body and feel the texture of the curtains. Feel the softness of the yellow cloth.

So be curious. Decide to see what's below the curtains. Observe the place where the curtains meet the windowsill. Pay close attention to small details of objects around the kitchen.

Now walk to the door. Touch the doorknob. Notice what it looks like in design and color. Before turning it, however, say, "On the other side of the door the Inner Master is waiting." Open the door. Sure enough, he's there. He looks like his photo. His eyes, too, show the familiar love and warmth.

"Are you ready?" he asks. "Let's take a walk outside."

You and Wah Z (my spiritual name) take a walk and admire the sights along the way. Strike up a conversation with Wah Z. Forget the heavy spiritual topics for now. Point out the beauty of a flower, for example, or the melodic song of a bird.

When you want to return to your physical body at rest in the kitchen chair, tell him so.

"Wah Z, may we go back to the kitchen? I want to see myself in the chair." Then go inside to the kitchen. All through this experience, sing *HU* or your secret word.

When you enter the kitchen, look at your human body, then say, "See you later, Wah Z. I'm going to sit down in the chair and get myself together." (A bit of humor.)

Then end the spiritual exercise by opening your physical eyes.

When you repeat this technique, Soul becomes used to going beyond the material self. At first, this technique may start with the imagination, but in time Soul Travel becomes a reality. So give it a chance. One day you'll find yourself in a higher state of consciousness, exactly as you acted it out so many times in your imagination.

Thought and imagination are powerful allies.

Imagination Gone Wrong

The human consciousness is under the hand of the Kal, the negative power. It is a state of poor survival factors. But some people are even worse off than the general lot and bump into bad luck more often than seems their due. Why?

Mainly, it's from negative expectations. Each is a self-fulfilling prophecy, a walking disaster. You want to steer clear of such a one.

An example is the story of a young nurse. She faced a promising career at a hospital but was devastated to be fired for the habit of arriving at work late. Within a month or so, however, she found a new position. All seemed well at first.

It turned out to be a dreadful place to work. Other nurses took a strong dislike to her and used underhanded tricks to try to drive her out. Still, she hung on. But every day was a living hell. What had she done to deserve such raw treatment?

In fact, it was old karma burning off in preparation for her introduction to the teachings of ECK.

The conditions became worse. She further added to the problem by letting her imagination look for an easy way out. She begged God for deliverance from earth. She wanted to die.

How much more negative is it possible to get?

However, God turned a deaf ear to her prayers.

She raised the ante. The next prayer said this: "Please, God, make me average." Perhaps the other nurses had turned up their noses at her because she was a nurse with superior habits and skills.

Nothing in her power would melt their wall of ice.

Her next step was to seek counseling. For a while, it looked as if the sessions might offer a hope of brighter things to come, but they never came. Stepping back, she saw that the counseling was running in circles. So she quit it. With no idea of a next best step, she nonetheless knew it was time to take charge of her own life.

The question was *how*.

Yet the decision to end counseling was a moment of truth. It changed her take on life from a negative accent to a positive one. Something would turn up. She just knew.

Then, a series of odd coincidences resulted in her creating new patterns of thought via self-help groups, books, and the like. A short while later, the teachings of ECK appeared in her life. She was quick to recognize the truth in them, because they held out the understanding she had sought for so long. There was indeed a pot of gold at the end of the rainbow.

About the same time, an inner experience from childhood made its reappearance, and it compelled her to take steps in a new, untried direction.

But notice how her new positive expectations turned things sunny-side up.

A doctor soon offered her a job on his staff. It was a dream position, in marked contrast to the past year and a half of misery. Yet old negative thoughts died hard. At one point, she had it in mind that her death would occur a few months down the road. Her husband used every means to explain that she was only seeing the demise of her old negative state of expectations. No physical death was in her cards.

And it turned out according to his positive expectations. She lives who once was dead in spirit.

Life's been no rose garden since the day she enrolled in ECKANKAR, but at least she now sees the reasons for and the spiritual benefits of her trials. Pain and heartache do cleanse Soul.

The name of the next spiritual exercise is the Imaginative technique. It'll help you develop positive expectations.

IMAGINATIVE TECHNIQUE

Soul Travel may occur in two general ways.

One form is the apparent movement of the Soul body through the planes of time and space. It is not, in fact, movement; Soul already exists on all planes. The appearance of movement, or travel, is simply the fixed states and conditions of the lower worlds coming into agreement with Soul.

That's the long and short of Soul Travel.

Let's introduce you to a prime imaginative technique for Soul Travel. Imagine a scene, and you can be there in the Soul body in the wink of an eye.

It may feel like a fast trip through space, and thus the idea of travel. However, Soul Travel is the process of changing the imagined setting around you to agree with spiritual reality.

To do this imaginative technique, take a scene from your storehouse of memories and try to change some activity in it. For example, imagine the sea lashing a beach. Now imagine the turbulent waters turning still, like water in a glass. Try this technique on other mental pictures. Change a grazing horse into a running horse, and so on.

When you do this technique, you may sometime notice the faint sensation of a rushing sound, like wind whistling in a tunnel. Again, there may be that sensation of fast movement.

However, all is as it should be.

Continue with the imaginative experiment, and sooner or later you'll find yourself in the mental picture of your creation, or in some other new one.

Have fun with this spiritual experiment.

A second form of Soul Travel mentioned at the beginning of this section is the expansion of consciousness. This form is the true state of revelation or enlightenment that one looks for in ECK. It is a natural offshoot of the Imaginative technique.

The Imaginative technique offers a deeper insight into the ways of the ECK (Holy Spirit) and into the means of gaining love, wisdom, and freedom for yourself.

What Is Spiritual Success?

An individual who starts the Spiritual Exercises of ECK may wonder, *What is success?* The answer could be within arm's reach.

Success is one's first meeting with the MAHANTA, the Living ECK Master—the Inner and Outer Master.

"The ECKist must always practice the Kundun, the presence, whether or not he can see this inner body of the Master," says *The Shariyat-Ki-SUGMAD, Books One & Two*. "It can, however, be noted many times by the outer manifestations of things such as the protection gained, the great feeling of love which surrounds the chela, the improvement of his welfare, and the attainment of spiritual knowledge. All is given freely to the ECKist after he has passed into the higher worlds via Soul Travel."

A few years ago, an ECKist met the MAHANTA right before awakening one morning. The Master handed him something. That was it. No more.

But at the ECK Worldwide Seminar that year, the Master appeared to him a second time, in a column of Blue Light. "I will walk every step with you," he said.

Then began an ordeal. The ECKist was diagnosed with cancer. As promised, the MAHANTA was beside him, to give comfort, aid, and guidance every step of the way through months of treatments. Five years later, the ECKist survives.

His fears are gone. He just wants others to know the importance of always keeping love and joy for all things in their hearts.

That, too, is spiritual success.

UNLOCKING TRUTH

The ECK always brings truth, but truth may come to each of us in different ways. The word, or mantra, you receive at an ECK initiation is your personal key to the ECK Life Stream, but you must experiment with this word.

At first you're apt to think the key is the wrong one, because it seems to open nothing. Work through this initial stage of preparation with a spiritual exercise. Use the creative technique that follows:

Chant *HU* or your secret word, and imagine it emblazoned upon a golden key. Fit this key into the lock of a door. Swing open the door. There, do you see?

The Light and Sound of God fill the room beyond.

And if that technique should run its course, try a new approach. The key is still OK, but perhaps the lock has frozen. So warm the key with a match or lighter, then insert it into the lock. It will now turn. Also experiment with lubricating oil. But whatever you do, keep working with your imagination and your personal word. Then watch! The MAHANTA will feed you new ideas to try.

These exercises develop your creative powers.

In any case, a new spiritual experience of some sort will always turn up. There is always a way. This principle will stand you in good stead with any stalemate. So always look for a way out.

And be assured that your spiritual unfoldment is ever on track.

Which Came First?

An old puzzler is the question Which came first, the chicken or the egg?

There's no big mystery about it. To my mind, the egg came first. The parents of the first chick were not quite chickens, but close. This one egg in the nest had a *mutant* chick inside. In time, some of those mutant genes mixed with those of other not-quite-a-chicken-yet fowl, and thus evolved today's chicken.

Likewise, Which comes first, dream travel or Soul Travel?

There's no pat answer.

LM of Las Vegas, Nevada, tells of an occasion when Soul Travel was the first half of a two-part experience that later continued in the dream state. And then, the dream trailed over to the following night.

One morning as she did her spiritual exercise in bed, Soul Travel whisked her to a beach to meet the ECK Masters Rebazar Tarzs and Wah Z (my spiritual name). She'd been having a problem with a mental barrier. It made the path of ECK more difficult, because it had drawn her to the power of the mind instead of love. All attempts to control or overcome the mind had failed.

Love, a lesson she was to learn from the Masters, takes little effort in comparison to the energy used in a power field. Love dances, while the mind plods in heavy boots.

LM asked Wah Z and Rebazar's advice on how to be free of her rigid mind.

"My mind is holding on to old ideas and thoughts," she said. "I let them go, surrender to the ECK, and soon they return again, pestering me."

The three continued along the edge of the water. Soon the force field of an invisible barrier blocked their way. It was an absolute bar to further progress. She likened the barrier to an enormous sheet of plastic wrapping. First, tapping her creative powers to find a way past it, she charged at it, to break through. But the barrier held. Like a spring, it shot her backward through the air at a tremendous speed.

Next, LM thought of using an ordinary pin. One appeared in her hand, so she pricked the sheet; and the whole barrier collapsed. Now the path was clear. They could resume their walk.

During this test, the two Masters had kept in the background as watchers. She handled the impasse herself.

The three thus continued along the beach.

Now there came a zone of dense white mist, which she later determined was a screen of sorts to guard the approach to the Etheric Plane. This plane is at the top of the Mental world.

So with no anchor points from which to tell direction in the white mist, she faced a whiteout. Uncertain of the right way to proceed, LM nevertheless hurried on. The two ECK Masters stayed close to offer aid and protection if needed. As she entered the mist, she hit a second barrier. This time, of course, the pin failed. There's no way to prick a mist and deflate it.

But she thought of something else.

The word *Baju* came to mind, and she knew it to be a charged spiritual word that allows entrance to the Etheric world. She spoke it; the mist cleared. So the small party advanced. Ahead, there appeared a round temple where the ECK Master Lai Tsi taught. The venerable Master came out to greet them. (Lai Tsi had once lived and served the SUGMAD in ancient China.)

He guided LM to a room where about ten other students were seated.

Lai Tsi said, "You've all been called here to work on a specific problem. You can go anywhere on this plane to solve it."

Then he turned to LM.

"You can come here as often as it is necessary to get control over the mind."

* * *

The morning she sat down to write about this experience in her initiate report to the MAHANTA, the Living ECK Master, she'd picked up *The Shariyat-Ki-SUGMAD*, Book One. Flipping the pages at random, she stopped at a certain place.

Here's the passage that met her eyes:

"Those who listen to the MAHANTA and obey with love in their hearts shall find love everywhere. They shall receive the love of God and shall abide in the love of the Living ECK Master."

LM, thanks to the ECK Masters, had the support she needed to control her mind and free the power of love.

In the end, it hardly matters whether dream travel or Soul Travel comes first. But it is of prime importance to catch the spiritual lessons that accompany them.

Now let's go on to the next spiritual exercise.

BEST SLEEPING TECHNIQUE FOR SOUL TRAVEL

There are three main steps to prepare yourself for Soul Travel in the dream state:

1. Arrange your schedule to get as much sleep as needed to be fresh in the morning.

2. A few minutes before bedtime, read from one of the ECK books to signal your intent to pursue spiritual activity during sleep. Good choices are *The Shariyat-Ki-SUGMAD, Books One & Two* or *Stranger by the River*.
3. Then contemplate upon the image of the MAHANTA, the Living ECK Master. In this spiritual exercise, give an invitation to the Master like this: "I welcome you into my heart as my home. Please enter it as my guest."

    Then go to sleep as usual, but leave the Eye of Soul (located a bit above and between the eyebrows) alert to the coming of the teacher. Look for him, because he is always with you.

The Daily Routine of Spiritual Exercises

Soul's recognition of Itself comes by daily practice of the Spiritual Exercises of ECK. A true knowledge of the forces of God is in them, not in books.

Rebazar Tarzs once said, "I have never valued word-knowledge which is set down in books. This leads only to mental confusion and not to such practices as the Spiritual Exercises of ECK which bring actual realization of truth."

* * *

One's success with Soul Travel hinges upon a daily routine. Early in the morning is the best time for a spiritual exercise since the day is fresh, but your family or work schedule may dictate another hour. But do a contemplation every day, at a time convenient for you.

MJD of Texas is a willing servant of God's love to all life, both inner and outer. She says, "Use me as you will."

So it's no wonder to learn of her success with Soul Travel. In fact, the ECK Masters always come to reveal more advanced and better methods. These are the secret teachings.

She's found that doing the spiritual exercise at the same hour each morning pays off. (Writers, artists, and inventors often report the same spur to their creative efforts.) One needs to set a time and place in which the Holy Spirit may flow unhindered into an expectant heart and ready mind.

So, an example of Soul Travel from MJD is the following story.

Peddar Zaskq (Paul Twitchell's spiritual name), Rebazar Tarzs, and Wah Z came to give her tips on a new and easier way to Soul Travel. Peddar said to try breathing through a single nostril.

Here is what happened:

MJD was suddenly in the family's game room in the Soul body. The room is a choice spot to do her spiritual exercises, and there she favors her husband's recliner. In the Soul body, she tried to leave the room through a window. The exit, however, was through a wall. An instant later, though, she was back in the chair, with the three ECK Masters seated alongside.

This was certainly a low-key experience. Still, it filled her with a warm and comforting love.

* * *

A note is due here. New Soul Travelers sometimes worry about getting back into the physical body. That's the easy part. Soul is like a ball at the end of a rubber band, for It snaps right back in the moment the individual loses his focus. It's easy to do. Once he's free of the body, it feels so good and natural.

"Why, there's nothing to this," he says. "I've done this lots of times before."

And just that quick, the experience is over, to his great chagrin, for he ponders all the things he would have liked to see and do.

* * *

Then MJD awoke in her physical body and recorded the event. After that, she followed a practice of reading a short passage from a selected book, *The Shariyat-Ki-Sugmad*. (The words, you will find, give an added dimension to any experience.)

MJD is grateful for the love and aid of the ECK Masters. Their attention, she knows, speeds her on the passage home.

FIRST LANDMARKS
OF SOUL TRAVEL

One way to leave the body via Soul Travel is to lie down after dinner when you are drowsy.

Plan on a five-minute nap. Then watch the process of falling asleep. If you try the exercise with your mate, agree to meet outside the body a few moments later. Now watch. Try to catch the moment that your mate was free of the physical body in a spray of radiant light and entered the next higher spiritual zone.

Of course, you, the watcher, are already on the higher plane.

Everyone leaves the body upon falling asleep. It is a natural, though often unconscious, activity. In Soul Travel, the main difference is that we want to reach a higher state in full awareness.

The moment Soul leaves the human body, It may pass through a blue-grey zone right above the Physical Plane. It takes but a moment. This zone is one approach to the Astral Plane. The sensation of moving from the Physical to the Astral body is like a mild wind current slipping through a large iris.

The iris itself is the Spiritual Eye.

Soul thus enters this neutral zone of blue-grey tones in the Astral form, a sheath that glitters like a thousand sparkling stars.

This buffer zone is a corridor between the Physical and lower Astral Planes. It's like an underground silo for an enormous rocket and is perhaps two hundred feet in diameter and two thousand feet deep. The ceiling of this circular pocket is open to the heavens. There, you may see a brilliant canopy of white light. Again, you may see a night sky sprinkled with specks of twinkling stars, or some other scene.

Whatever scene displays in the opening of the vast ceiling, Soul rises toward it at a mighty speed, and then the real journey begins.

Most people start to recall a dream only after leaving this launching pad between the two worlds, after their arrival at some faraway destination on the Astral Plane.

Rebazar Tarzs Helps Her Soul Travel

A mother from the Netherlands felt tired one afternoon, so she lay down for a quick nap. She felt tired, yet restless. But sleep played cat and mouse with her until a lightbulb clicked on in her mind.

So she said, "MAHANTA, give me an experience."

In that instant, she felt an upward surge inside her. She rose high above her resting human self, passing ocean upon ocean in the worlds beyond. Finally, she became exhausted from trying to absorb the rapid changes around her.

Then, with no warning, fear seized her on this spiritual journey.

Am I dying? She wondered. *What will become of my young children?*

Despite these annoying fears, this Soul

Travel experience had a beautiful side. "Too sweet to stop," she said. The assurance of the ECK Masters' promise of spiritual protection must have come into play then, because the experience picked up where it had left off.

World upon world continued to flash by. Ever higher she soared, into the very canopy of heaven, beyond the limitless blue and into an arena of breathless whiteness.

This white place was the Ocean of Love and Mercy. She'd come for a foretaste of God's home. There, she found a fountain of lights, in a circle, formed like a shrine. This round fountain of light bathed her in its glory. She felt a deep, satisfying thrill of joy.

But the next instant, her physical eyes opened to the familiar sights and sounds of her own home.

The grand journey was over.

Still heavy with sleep, she glanced at the clock. It said 4:45 p.m. Only a short nap?

But then something, rather someone, caught her eye—the figure of a man. It was the ECK Master Rebazar Tarzs. He had guided her on this Soul Travel adventure to let her taste of God's holy temple, her true home. Now it all came flooding back. During the experience itself, though, she had been very aware of his company. Once she'd overcome the sudden rush of fear, that is.

In Soul Travel experiences prior to this one, she says, she'd never left the house.

"Now all doubt I have about ECK is totally gone," says this enlightened mom.

Two points: first, she had but to ask the MAHANTA for an experience during a nap. Second, only a pure heart, free of dross, may approach the SUGMAD (God).

CALISTHENICS

For this technique sit on the floor. Shut your eyes and stretch out your legs in front of you. Take a deep breath. Then reach for your toes with your fingertips. Stretch only as far as you can short of straining; there is no point in overtaxing your muscles with a spiritual exercise.

At the same time chant "SUGMAD" *(SOOG-mahd)*.

Sing each syllable in a long and drawn-out fashion. Leaning forward, chant the first syllable, "SUG." Then return slowly to the upright position and sing "MAD."

This exercise opens the consciousness for Soul to visit the higher worlds. Do this exercise for seven repetitions, then take a short rest. End the exercise with five more repetitions.

Should a Soul Travel experience result, lie down and go with it.

And, of course, the Calisthenics technique is only for someone used to physical exercise, and with the approval of his doctor. The ECK writings have a lot of other Soul Travel exercises for those who are out of shape.

A Reality Check

Sandy, an Australian, was listening to the ECK recording "If God Is God, Then Who Are You?" A point made on the recording was that "the flying through space" experiences were a great lark. But to what end?

What benefit would such an experience afford anyone in a spiritual sense if that were the gist of it?

The Master's talk on the tape stirred old memories. Sandy had indeed enjoyed such flying experiences. They were a pleasure. But what made them stand out was the spiritual insights they brought, not just the freedom of inner flight.

Sandy's first attempts at flying while out of the body were like those of a young chicken: clumsy and exploratory. She tried harder. Despite more effort, she traveled a shorter distance still.

The MAHANTA's inner voice said, "Don't be so heavy-handed."

Following his advice, she began to lift gently upward. Soon she had the confidence to maintain the gentle attention it takes to stay aloft. Now she soared in the air. Carried away by exhilaration, she tried experiments like diving and cartwheels.

What a wonderful time!

But then came a reality check.

An inner nudge from the MAHANTA broke in on her aerobatics. "It's fine to have a good time," he said. "But with it must come a duty of service." The increase of spiritual powers carries with it a responsibility to turn those skills to service for others. The whole aim of unfoldment, you see, is that one day we may become a Coworker with God.

Sandy is grateful for all the insights won through the Spiritual Exercises of ECK.

The Shariyat-Ki-SUGMAD, Book Two, illuminates the big picture. It says: "ECK is the Audible Life Stream, the essence of the SUGMAD, the Holy Spirit, and the science of God-Realization. It grows out of the experience of Soul Travel into the state of religious awareness, which the subject gains at his own volition via the Spiritual Exercises of ECKANKAR."

The state of religious awareness!

That's where Sandy's reality check will lead to, in the course of joyous acts of service to others.

The two go hand in hand.

THE BLUE CURTAIN OF GOD

The first part of this spiritual exercise is to awaken the seeing power of Soul.

Find a time to sit or lie down for ten to twenty minutes when you will not be disturbed. Shut your eyes, but imagine a dark-blue curtain on the wall before you. The first few days, expect to see only the rich blue curtain. Later, some color of the Light of God will shine from it.

The second part of this exercise is to sharpen your spiritual hearing.

While looking at the blue curtain, begin to sing the word *HU* (pronounced like the word *hue*), an old name for God that saints have praised for thousands of years. After a few minutes, sing *HU* within yourself, making no audible sound. Continue a few minutes, then stop.

Sit quietly. Keep gazing at the royal-blue curtain before you. Listen to every sound, including those that come in from outside. Among them may be a true Sound, one from the ECK, the Holy Spirit.

One more thing: Throughout this short exercise, fill your heart with love for God.

* * *

Why pray, meditate, or contemplate? Certainly, the reason must be for something other than a materialistic gain or advantage. This thing called life is your pursuit. Each must make his own way to truth, on his own path and in his own time.

The route of this quest is both a unique and solitary one. Yet all creation awaits the awakening of each individual Soul.

So why pray, meditate, or contemplate, or turn to the practice and understanding of, say, dreams?

It is so you may flourish in Spirit. Life's richness is all around you if you would but awaken, open your Spiritual Eye. Should you wish help in this life-changing, challenging pursuit, you have but to ask. The Inner Master will come.

Scan to learn more about HU.

6
By the Way

In *Stranger by the River*, "Jewels of Wisdom," ECK Master Rebazar Tarzs imparts a great secret to the seeker.

"The way of love is better than wisdom and understanding," he says, "for with love you can have all."

Short and sweet.

In reading to this point you've stayed the journey. Yet the greater one is still to come. Perhaps you now see that past lives, dreams, and Soul Travel are all a major part of the spiritual journey. However, none alone is its full substance, for beyond them lie the heart and spirit of life. That something is God's love.

The principle of all existence rests upon a single truth: Soul exists because God loves It.

Stop and think. If that is true, then the created is bound to the Creator. That is the secret of life. Love is all. There is nothing else. The people, places, and things about us that we take for granted are all a manifestation of God's love.

But sorrow, deprivation, loneliness, and every other expression of a negative nature are all signs of a temporary separation from God's love.

The Spiritual Exercises of ECK will help the sincere in heart find the source of divine love. This effort of returning home must come of conscious effort. It's the reason for the Spiritual Exercises of ECK.

Other Souls have trod this timeless path to God in ages past. An untold multitude. Thousands more seek it now.

Are the ECK teachings for you? Only your heart can say.

Earth is a school. It is a place to study and learn about goodness, service, and every other supreme quality by way of the lessons of everyday life. Then your Spiritual

Eye will open to the Spirit of God shining in every living thing.

Think how the history of mankind might read if more enlightened Souls were to mix among the masses who stumble about in spiritual gloom.

Yet for all that, the spiritual path of ECK is an individual quest. Each person must walk it by himself.

It comes down to free will, doesn't it?

Whether or not the hour and season are right for you to set foot to the most grand adventure in life, I am sure that the words in these pages will forever change you. You will never again be the same. Soul has heard and is yearning to go home.

To find love and spiritual freedom—that's the purpose of our incarnations.

Good dreams to you, and many happy journeys.

About the Author

Award-winning author, teacher, and spiritual guide Sri Harold Klemp helps seekers reach their full potential.

He is the MAHANTA, the Living ECK Master and spiritual leader of ECKANKAR, the Path of Spiritual Freedom. He is the latest in a long line of spiritual Adepts who have served throughout history in every culture of the world.

Sri Harold teaches creative spiritual practices that enable anyone to achieve life mastery and gain inner peace and contentment. His messages are relevant to today's spiritual needs and resonate with every generation.

Sri Harold's body of work includes more than one hundred books, which have been translated into eighteen languages and won multiple awards. The miraculous, true-life stories he shares lift the veil between heaven and earth.

In his groundbreaking memoir, *Autobiography of a Modern Prophet*, he reveals secrets to spiritual success gleaned from his personal journey into the heart of God.

Find your own path to true happiness, wisdom, and love in Sri Harold Klemp's inspired writings.

Next Steps in Spiritual Exploration

- Learn more about **Soul Travel**:

Soul Travel

* * *

- Visit **Eckankar.org** to explore a vast array of spiritual resources to aid you in your search for truth.

- Get **books** on a wide variety of spiritual topics at ECKANKAR's books website: **ECKBooks.org**.

- **Call or write us:**

ECKANKAR
PO Box 2000
Chanhassen, MN 55317-2000 USA
(952) 380-2222

ECKANKAR'S
Spiritual Living Courses

Go higher, further, deeper with your spiritual experiences!

ECKANKAR offers enrollment in the Spiritual Living Courses for Self-Discovery and God-Discovery. This dynamic program of inner and outer study unlocks the divine love and wisdom within you. It offers step-by-step advances in enlightenment through spiritual initiations.

From the first day, you can have direct experience with the God Current and begin to meet life's challenges on the highest possible ground.

You will enjoy monthly lessons (also available online) from the spiritual leader of

ECKANKAR, Sri Harold Klemp, creative spiritual practices for daily life, and the quarterly *Mystic World* publication. Optional classes with like-hearted Souls are available in many areas.

Here's a sampling of titles from the first course:

- In Soul You Are Free
- Reincarnation—Why You Came to Earth Again
- The Master Principle
- The God Worlds—Where No One Has Gone Before?

Learn more about
ECKANKAR's Spiritual Living Courses.

For Further Reading
By Harold Klemp

ECKANKAR—Key to Dreams

Unlock the power of your dreams.

Dreams are a spiritual gold mine. They can offer glimpses into past lives, soothe a broken heart, and settle the deepest questions in life. But it takes a certain knowledge to reach the inner worlds.

In *ECKANKAR—Key to Dreams*, Sri Harold Klemp, the spiritual leader of ECKANKAR and a leading expert on dreams, shows how anyone can enrich their life through the dynamic art of dreaming.

He offers spiritual exercises to

- recall dreams,
- dream consciously,
- resolve karma, and
- get answers on health, love, finances, and more.

Unlock the full potential of your dreams and experience a life of greater adventure. Start your dream study today!

Eckankar—Key to Past Lives

Ever wonder about reincarnation?

Have I lived before? Are there past-life roots to my fears? Did I really fall in love at *first* sight? Why do bad things happen to good people?

In *Eckankar—Key to Past Lives*, Sri Harold Klemp, the spiritual leader of Eckankar and a leading authority on past lives, answers age-old questions about reincarnation.

He shows that, without past-life regression or hypnosis, you can naturally reduce fear of dying (and living). Discover past-life recall through spiritual exercises (a higher form of guided meditation) and a study of dreams.

Just a few of the fascinating, true stories in this book:

- A businessman uses contemplation (a way to access inner wisdom) to resolve karma with his horrible boss.
- A woman's memory of the *Titanic* disaster reveals a karmic debt that explains this lifetime's tragic losses.
- A man, torn between his college sweetheart and a girl he just met, remembers a past life about whom to marry.

Bring more harmony to your life by untangling karmic webs from long ago. An extraordinary read!

To get these and other books to ignite your spiritual life, visit **Eckankar's page on Amazon** via the QR Code below.

See **Eckankar books** on Amazon.

Glossary

Words set in SMALL CAPS are defined elsewhere in this glossary.

Blue Light How the MAHANTA often appears in the inner worlds to the CHELA or seeker.

chela A spiritual student of ECKANKAR and the LIVING ECK MASTER.

ECK The Life Force, Holy Spirit, or Audible Life Current which sustains all life.

ECKANKAR *EHK-ahn-kahr* The Path of Spiritual Freedom. Also known as the Ancient Science of SOUL TRAVEL. A truly spiritual way of life for the individual in modern times. The teachings provide a framework for anyone to explore their own spiritual experiences. Established by PAUL TWITCHELL, the modern-day founder, in 1965. The word means Coworker with God.

ECK Masters Spiritual Masters who can assist and protect people in their spiritual studies and travels. The ECK Masters are from a long line of God-Realized SOULS who know the responsibility that goes with spiritual freedom.

God-Realization The state of God Consciousness. Complete and conscious awareness of God. To love as God loves.

Harold Klemp The present MAHANTA, the LIVING ECK MASTER. Sri Harold Klemp became the MAHANTA, the Living ECK Master in 1981. His spiritual name is WAH Z.

HU *HYOO* An ancient, sacred name for God. It is a carrier of love between God and SOUL and can be sung aloud or silently to oneself to align with the God Current. It is the Sound of Soul.

initiations Steps of enlightenment. The ECK initiation is a sacred ceremony in which the spiritual student is linked to the Sound and Light of God for greater wisdom and love.

Karma, Law of The Law of Cause and Effect, action and reaction, justice, retribution, and reward, which applies to the lower or psychic worlds: the Physical, Astral, Causal, Mental, and Etheric PLANES.

Living ECK Master The spiritual leader of ECKANKAR. He leads SOUL back to God. He teaches in the physical world as the Outer Master, in the dream state as the Dream Master, and in the spiritual worlds as the Inner Master. SRI HAROLD KLEMP became the MAHANTA, the Living ECK Master in 1981.

MAHANTA An expression of the Spirit of God that is always with you. Sometimes seen as a

Blue Light or Blue Star or in the form of the Mahanta, the Living ECK Master. The highest state of God Consciousness on earth, only embodied in the Living ECK Master. He is the Living Word.

Paul Twitchell An American ECK Master who brought the modern teachings of Eckankar to the world through his writings and lectures. His spiritual name is Peddar Zaskq.

Peddar Zaskq The spiritual name for Paul Twitchell, the modern-day founder of Eckankar and the Mahanta, the Living ECK Master from 1965 to 1971.

planes Levels of existence, such as the Physical, Astral, Causal, Mental, Etheric, and Soul Planes.

Rebazar Tarzs A Tibetan ECK Master known as the Torchbearer of Eckankar in the lower worlds.

Satsang A class in which students of ECK discuss a monthly lesson from Eckankar.

Self-Realization Soul recognition. The entering of Soul into the Soul Plane and there beholding Itself as pure Spirit. A state of Seeing, Knowing, and Being.

Shariyat-Ki-Sugmad Way of the Eternal; the sacred scriptures of Eckankar. The scriptures are comprised of twelve volumes in the spiritual worlds. The first two were transcribed from the inner PLANES by PAUL TWITCHELL, modern-day founder of ECKANKAR.

Soul The True Self, an individual, eternal spark of God. The inner, most sacred part of each person. Soul can see, know, and perceive all things. It is the creative center of Its own world.

Soul Travel The expansion of consciousness. The ability of SOUL to transcend the physical body and travel into the spiritual worlds of God. Soul Travel is taught only by the LIVING ECK MASTER. It helps people unfold spiritually and can provide proof of the existence of God and life after death.

Sound and Light of ECK The Holy Spirit. The two aspects through which God appears in the lower worlds. People can experience the Sound and Light by looking and listening within themselves and through SOUL TRAVEL.

Spiritual Exercises of ECK Daily practices for direct, personal experience with the God Current. Creative techniques using contemplation and the singing of sacred words to bring the higher awareness of SOUL into daily life.

Sri A title of spiritual respect, similar to reverend or pastor, used for those who have attained the Kingdom of God. In ECKANKAR, it is reserved for the MAHANTA, the LIVING ECK MASTER.

SUGMAD *SOOG-mahd* A sacred name for God. It is the source of all life, neither male nor female, the Ocean of Love and Mercy.

Temples of Golden Wisdom Golden Wisdom Temples found on the various PLANES—from the Physical to the Anami Lok. CHELAS of ECKANKAR visit these temples in the SOUL body to be educated in the divine knowledge. Sections of the SHARIYAT-KI-SUGMAD, the sacred teachings of ECK, are kept at these temples.

Wah Z *WAH zee* The spiritual name of SRI HAROLD KLEMP. It means the secret doctrine. It is his name in the spiritual worlds.

For more explanations of ECKANKAR terms, see *ECKopedia: The ECKANKAR Lexicon*, by Harold Klemp.